Knowledge
in a Nutshell

D0101282

Charles Reichblum

arpr, inc.

Paperbacks

KNOWLEDGE IN A NUTSHELL

Copyright © 1994 by Charles Reichblum.

To order additional copies of this book, call 1-800-633-3082.
Quantity discounts available.

ISBN: 0-9660991-8-4 (previously ISBN 0-312-95349-6)

Printed in the United States of America by Geyer Printing Co. Pgh., PA

arpr, inc., Paperbacks edition / October 1999

10 9 8 7 6 5 4

To Audrey, Bob, Bill, Diane, and Amalie
    for their support and interest in
    all these facts and stories.

To Rachel, Justin, Noah, and Clarissa
    for their inspiration.

To Barbara and Angela
    for all that typing.

TABLE OF CONTENTS

Preface

Some kids collected baseball cards. Others collected stamps. But when I was a helper at a radio station newsroom at age fourteen, with daily access to the news wire and many newspapers, I started collecting facts and stories that surprised me, or taught me something interesting, or were fun to know.

One day there was a story on the Fourth of July, and deep down in the text there was a note that three of the first five U.S. Presidents had—by coincidence—all died on July 4. I clipped that and saved it.

Over the years, I kept adding interesting facts to my collection every time I heard one, or read one, or dug one out in my research.

But how many really were true? When I began my own news service, Century Features, in 1959, I started checking and verifying all those facts I had.

I used three criteria for the ones I wanted to keep: Were they accurate, were they informative, and were they interesting?

This book is the result of a now fifty-year collection of these facts and stories.

One

U.S. Presidents

The amazing coincidence of presidential deaths on Independence Day

Three of the first five U.S. Presidents all died on July 4.

The second President, John Adams, died in Quincy, Massachusetts, on July 4, 1826.

The third President, Thomas Jefferson, died in Charlottesville, Virginia, on the same day, in the same year as Adams, July 4, 1826.

And the fifth President, James Monroe, died in New York City on July 4, 1831.

He was the father and the son of U.S. President

John Harrison of North Bend, Ohio, was unique in American history. He was both the father *and* the son of a U.S. President.

His father was William Henry Harrison, who was elected President of the United States in 1840.

His son was Benjamin Harrison, who became President of the U.S. in 1888.

Although John Harrison never became President like his father and his son, he did become a U.S. congressman from Ohio from 1852 to 1857.

Did the U.S. always have a President?

The United States once went thirteen years *without* a President.

The U.S. was formed in 1776, but George Washington did not take office as first President until 1789—and yet during those thirteen years, the U.S. got off the ground, won a war, and functioned as a successful nation.

U.S. President elected by one vote

The presidential election of 1876 between Rutherford Hayes and Samuel Tilden gave neither man the required electoral votes. So the election was thrown into Congress, where a fifteen-man commission was chosen to vote on the winner.

Hayes won 8–7, and thereby became U.S. President by the margin of one vote.

Tell the President he's not the President

One of the most unusual election nights in American history occurred November 7, 1916, when many people went to bed thinking Charles Evans Hughes was elected U.S. President over Woodrow Wilson.

Hughes, himself, went to bed at one A.M.—convinced he had won.

However, late returns changed the outcome, and gave the election to Wilson.

A reporter called Hughes's room to get his reaction. A Hughes aide who answered the phone said, "The President is asleep." The reporter said, "When the President wakes up, tell him he's not the President."

Roosevelt was the youngest President

The youngest person ever to be President of the United States was not John Kennedy, as many believe.

The youngest President was Theodore Roosevelt. Roosevelt was forty-two when he became President in 1901.

Kennedy was the second-youngest President. He was forty-three when he was inaugurated in 1961.

Bill Clinton ranks as the third-youngest President, inaugurated at age forty-six.

First woman nominated for U.S. President

It wasn't in any recent year that the first woman was nominated to run for President of the United States.

It happened in 1872.

Victoria Claflin Woodhull of New York was nominated by the Equal Rights Party. Her running mate was the first black ever nominated for U.S. Vice President, Frederick Douglass. The election was won by Ulysses Grant.

The first woman nominated for President by a major party was Senator Margaret Chase Smith of Maine. Smith's name was placed in nomination at the Republican convention in 1964, and she received 27 votes on the first ballot, which was won by Barry Goldwater.

President Bill Clinton's name wasn't Bill Clinton

Bill Clinton's name originally was Bill Blythe.

His father and mother were William and Virginia Blythe.

His father died, and his mother later married Roger Clinton.

At age sixteen, the future President changed his name from Bill Blythe to Bill Clinton.

Father of country no father

Ironically, the man called "the Father of the Country"— George Washington—was never a father himself.

Washington and his wife, Martha, had no children of their own.

Five other U.S. Presidents also had no children: James Madison, Andrew Jackson, James Polk, James Buchanan, and Warren Harding.

At the other end of the scale, the President who had the greatest number of children was John Tyler. Tyler had fifteen children.

Kennedy, Lincoln similarities topped off as Kennedy is shot in Lincoln

There were many startling similarities in the assassinations of Presidents Kennedy and Lincoln.

Both were shot on a Friday.

The names Lincoln and Kennedy each have seven letters. The assassins' names—John Wilkes Booth and Lee Harvey Oswald—each have fifteen letters.

Booth was born in 1839, Oswald in 1939.

Lincoln was elected in 1860, Kennedy in 1960.

Lincoln and Kennedy were both succeeded by men named Johnson—Andrew Johnson, who was born in 1808; and Lyndon Johnson, who was born in 1908.

Lincoln's secretary was named Kennedy, and Kennedy's secretary was named Lincoln.

To top it off, the make of car in which Kennedy was riding when he was shot was . . . a Lincoln.

Last non-Democrat, non-Republican to be President

Who was the last U.S. President who was neither a Democrat nor a Republican?

He was the thirteenth President, Millard Fillmore, who served from 1850 to 1853. Fillmore was a member of the Whig Party.

Since then, the closest any non-Democrat or non-Republican has come to the presidency was Theodore Roosevelt. Roosevelt ran on the Progressive Party ticket in 1912 and beat the Republican—William Howard Taft—but lost to the Democrat, Woodrow Wilson.

Do you have to be a lawyer to be President?

Twenty-six of the forty-one men who have served as President of the United States were lawyers.

The fifteen Presidents who were not lawyers:

George Bush, Ronald Reagan, Jimmy Carter, Lyndon Johnson, John Kennedy, Dwight Eisenhower, Harry Truman, Herbert Hoover, Warren Harding, Theodore Roosevelt, Ulysses Grant, Andrew Johnson, Zachary Taylor, William Harrison, and George Washington.

He won the popular vote—but never became President

Samuel Tilden ran for President of the United States in 1876, and got more popular votes than anyone else that year—but Tilden never became President.

Tilden received 4,284,757 votes, while runner-up Rutherford Hayes got 4,033,950.

But neither man had the required 185 electoral votes. Tilden had 184 and Hayes had 165, with 20 votes in dispute over the eligibility of electors in four states.

A special congressional committee was chosen to decide the election. They debated until March 2, 1877, just three days before Inauguration Day. From the time of the general election in November 1876, until March 2, 1877, the nation didn't know who would be President.

Finally, the fifteen-member committee voted 8–7 on strict party lines to award the election to Hayes.

Tilden was never nominated again.

U.S. Presidents didn't wear pants

None of the first three U.S. Presidents regularly wore trousers or long pants as men do today.

The first three Presidents—George Washington, John

Adams, and Thomas Jefferson—usually wore breeches or knickers.

The style began to change in the early 1800s.

The first U.S. President to switch from breeches to long pants was James Madison.

Biggest losers in presidential elections

Of all the people who've ever run for President of the United States on a major-party ticket, which one suffered the worst defeat?

If you count the biggest popular vote differential for a runner-up, the answer is George McGovern. He lost by over 17 million votes to Richard Nixon in 1972 (47,165,234 to 29,170,774).

The biggest loser in electoral vote differential was Alf Landon, who lost by 515 electoral votes to Franklin Roosevelt in 1936 (523 to 8).

Lightweight President

There was one President of the United States who weighed less than 100 pounds when he was in office.

He was James Madison, the smallest U.S. President. Madison's height, to go with his less than 100-pound weight, was five feet four inches.

The tallest President was Abraham Lincoln who stood six feet four inches. The heaviest was William Howard Taft, who, at times, weighed over 300 pounds.

This President hardly ever got started

There was one U.S. President who lasted only thirty-two days in office.

He was the ninth President, William Henry Harrison.

Harrison caught a cold during his outdoor inauguration ceremonies on March 4, 1841, and he died of pneumonia on April 4, 1841, at the age of sixty-eight.

Harrison was the only U.S. President who never signed a bill or performed any significant presidential action.

Harrison became the first U.S. President to die in office, and he was succeeded by his Vice President, John Tyler.

Brother vs. brother for President

Two brothers once ran against each other for President of the United States.

In 1796, Charles Pinckney and his younger brother Thomas, of South Carolina, both received electoral votes for President at the same time.

Neither made it—John Adams won the election—but it was the first and only time in U.S. history that two brothers got electoral votes for President in the same election.

Two Presidents have no opposition

The United States had two Presidents who were so popular nobody could be found to run against them.

Nobody ran against George Washington. And in the election of 1820, nobody ran against James Monroe.

That time was called "the era of good feeling," and Monroe won his second term without any opposition.

All members of the Electoral College, with one exception, voted for Monroe. William Plumer of New Hampshire cast his vote for John Quincy Adams, who was not a candidate. Plumer wasn't opposed to Monroe, but felt no one other than George Washington should be honored with a unanimous election.

Only two U.S. Presidents were seventy years old

Of all the Presidents in U.S. history, surprisingly, only two served at age seventy or older.

Ronald Reagan was the oldest President. He took office at age sixty-nine and left at age seventy-seven.

The only other seventy-year-old President was Dwight Eisenhower, who started his first term at age sixty-two and ended his second term at age seventy.

Eight other Presidents began their terms in their sixties, but none of those eight was still in office at age seventy.

Franklin Roosevelt, who was President for twelve years, longer than anyone else, took office at age fifty-one and died at age sixty-three.

Roosevelt's wife and mother die on same day

In a strange coincidence, President Theodore Roosevelt's mother and wife both died—from completely unrelated causes—on the same day, in the same year.

Roosevelt's mother, Mrs. Martha Roosevelt, died on February 14, 1884, of typhoid fever. Roosevelt's wife, Alice, died giving birth to a child the same day, February 14, 1884—Valentine's Day.

The unqualified President

Every U.S. President—except one—gained experience either as a member of Congress, a governor of a state, a famous army general, or in a high-level government job.

The only President who had none of those qualifications was the 21st President, Chester Arthur.

Arthur had been Collector for the Port of New York—and he was fired from that job. He practiced law off and on and dabbled in politics, becoming a delegate to the Republican Convention in 1880. They nominated him as Vice President, and he became President upon the death of James Garfield.

Despite his lack of experience, Arthur turned out to be a fairly effective President, although he was not nominated to run for a second term.

Big state of California produces only one U.S. President—while little Vermont has two

Only one U.S. President was born in California, the most populous state. That was Richard Nixon.

Of course, California has led the nation in population only in recent times, but it's an oddity that Vermont, which has always been sparsely populated, has produced two Presidents—Chester Arthur and Calvin Coolidge.

Virginia still leads in the production of Presidents. Eight Presidents were born in Virginia, including four of the first five—George Washington, Thomas Jefferson, James Madison, and James Monroe. The other Virginia Presidents were William Henry Harrison, John Tyler, Zachary Taylor, and Woodrow Wilson.

Ohio ranks next with seven. Then comes Massachusetts and New York, with four each.

Who would have predicted success for Ulysses Grant?

Perhaps the most unlikely person ever to become President of the United States was Ulysses Grant, based on his early adult life.

Grant tried farming and failed; he worked in real estate and failed; he set up a store and failed. He went into the Army but was discharged for alcoholism.

At that point, who would have predicted that Grant would someday be President?

But then Grant got his life together. He reentered the

Army and went on to a successful military and political career. He was elected U.S. President in 1868.

No day of mourning for this President

John Tyler, the U.S. President from 1841 to 1845, died in 1862, in Richmond, Virginia. The Civil War was on at that time, and since Tyler lived in the South, President Lincoln took no official notice of Tyler's death.

There were no flags flown at half-staff, no announcement, no proclamation. John Tyler became the only U.S. President whose death was officially ignored.

Jailed man gets large vote for President

A man in jail once received almost one million votes for President of the United States.

It happened in the 1920 presidential election when Eugene Debs, who ran on a third-party Socialist ticket against Warren Harding and James Cox, received 919,799 votes.

Debs was in the Atlanta Penitentiary, serving a ten-year sentence for violating the Espionage Act. He had been convicted for opposition to U.S. entry in World War I.

Debs spent the entire presidential campaign in the penitentiary, but over 900,000 people voted for him.

Harding, who won the election, commuted Debs's sentence a year later, but Debs never regained his citizenship.

Presidential candidate didn't know he was nominated

Unbelievably, a man was once nominated to run for President of the United States—but he didn't know it.

It happened to Zachary Taylor, who was elected President in 1848.

Taylor was at a remote Army post during the nominating process. There was, of course, no telephone or telegraph then. Taylor was sent a letter, telling him of his nomination, but he refused the letter because it came postage due.

Taylor didn't find out he had been nominated for the presidency till a messenger came to tell him.

Last President to wear a mustache

No U.S. President for many years has worn a mustache.

The last President to wear a mustache on a daily basis was William Howard Taft, who was President from 1909 to 1913.

Thomas Dewey, who wore a mustache, almost made the presidency in 1948, but he was upset by Harry Truman. Truman wore no mustache.

The zero presidential jinx

Every U.S. President elected in a year ending in zero for 120 years—from 1840 to 1960—died in office.

Here are those Presidents and the years in which they

were elected: William Henry Harrison, 1840; Abraham Lincoln, 1860; James Garfield, 1880; William McKinley, 1900; Warren Harding, 1920; Franklin Roosevelt, 1940; John Kennedy, 1960.

The next President elected in a zero year was Ronald Reagan, in 1980. He barely missed an assassination attempt, survived through his term, and broke the jinx.

No school for this U.S. President

One President of the United States never went to school in his life.

He was the seventeenth President, Andrew Johnson.

Johnson went to work as an apprentice tailor when he was a young boy, and later opened a tailor shop. He was taught to read and write by Eliza McCardle when he was seventeen years old, and they married when he was nineteen.

He started his political career in Greeneville, Tennessee, serving as alderman and mayor.

Eventually he was elected to his state legislature and then became governor of Tennessee and a U.S. congressman.

Abraham Lincoln selected Johnson as Vice President, and he succeeded to the presidency on Lincoln's death.

Washington never lived in White House

The White House wasn't built yet when George Washington was President of the U.S. Where did America's first President live?

George Washington originally governed the country from New York City, and the first presidential mansion was located, oddly enough, on Cherry Street in New York.

The street was not named because of Washington's legendary connection with cherry trees. The street was named Cherry Street long before Washington moved there.

Washington, by the way, was the only U.S. President who never lived in the White House.

He ran for mayor and lost: he ran for President and won

Who would think a person who couldn't get elected mayor of his city could then get elected President of the United States?

That happened to Theodore Roosevelt.

Roosevelt ran for mayor of New York City in 1886, and lost.

He ran for President in 1904, and won.

President Gerald Ford was King

U.S. President Gerald Ford was born with a different name. His original name was Leslie King when he was born in Omaha, Nebraska, on July 14, 1913.

However, his mother and father divorced, and his mother then married a man named Gerald Ford of Grand Rapids, Michigan. Mr. Ford legally adopted Leslie King and gave him the name of Gerald Ford, Jr.

But for part of his life Ford was King.

President's first act is to go to sleep

Calvin Coolidge was U.S. Vice President in 1923, and he was home in Vermont when word came late at night that President Harding had died.

Coolidge was awakened and given the oath of office by his father, who was a justice of the peace.

Coolidge then performed his first act as President of the United States. He went right back to bed and, according to reports, slept soundly.

The election that ended in a dead heat

One election for President of the U.S. ended in a tie.

That was the election of 1800 between Thomas Jefferson and Aaron Burr.

Both Jefferson and Burr received the same number of electoral votes, 73.

In the case of an electoral tie, the Constitution says the House of Representatives must vote to break it.

The House chose Jefferson. And that's how Thomas Jefferson became President—in the only presidential election ending in a tie.

Mom couldn't vote for son to be President

For the first 156 years of the United States—from 1776 to 1932—no U.S. President had a mother who could vote for him.

The reason is that no woman anywhere in the country was eligible to vote in presidential elections until 1920, and the Presidents who were elected in 1920, 1924, and 1928 did not have mothers alive at that time.

Franklin Roosevelt in 1932 was the first President whose mother could vote for him.

The only President who came back four years later

Grover Cleveland was the 22nd U.S. President, serving from 1885 to 1889.

Then he ran for a second term, but lost to Benjamin Harrison. Harrison became the 23rd President.

However, Cleveland wasn't done. He challenged Harrison four years later—and won, becoming also the 24th President and the only President to serve in non-consecutive terms.

The most incredible campaign speech

On October 14, 1912, Theodore Roosevelt was running for President, and was about to make a speech in Milwaukee.

Suddenly, Roosevelt was shot in the chest. But he insisted on speaking.

He started the speech by saying, "Friends, I ask you to be very quiet and please excuse me from making a very long speech. You see, I have a bullet in my body. But it's nothing. I'll deliver this speech or die."

He spoke for fifty minutes, then went to a hospital and had the bullet removed.

The bullet had been partly deflected by a glass case

Roosevelt had in his pocket, but his shirt and coat were covered with blood as he spoke.

He survived.

Franklin Roosevelt can't carry home county

There's an old saying about a person not being a prophet in his own hometown, and that certainly applied to one of America's most famous Presidents, Franklin Roosevelt.

Roosevelt was a popular President. He was the only person elected President four times, but here's the unusual part:

Although he won each of his four national presidential elections by big margins, Roosevelt never carried his home county, Dutchess County in New York, in any of those elections.·

The only three-time loser on a major party ticket

Only one man in U.S. history was nominated by a major party to run for President three times and lost every time.

He was William Jennings Bryan.

The Democrats nominated Bryan in 1896, but he lost to the Republican, William McKinley.

The Democrats tried again in 1900, pitting Bryan against McKinley for a second time, but Bryan lost again.

After an eight-year hiatus, the Democrats turned to Bryan once more, running him against William Howard Taft in 1908. But Bryan made history by losing yet again.

Presidents used outhouses

The White House opened in 1800—but it didn't get indoor plumbing until 1833, when the seventh President, Andrew Jackson was in office.

That means the early Presidents, including John Adams, Thomas Jefferson, James Madison, James Monroe, and John Quincy Adams used the outhouse, which presumably was somewhere on the White House grounds.

Indoor plumbing wasn't all the White House didn't have in those days. There was no air-conditioning, electric light, or telephone either.

The lucky (unlucky) carnation

The 25th President, William McKinley, always wore what he considered a lucky red carnation in his lapel every day. But on September 6, 1901, on a trip to Buffalo, New York, he gave his carnation to a little girl. Later that day, McKinley, without his lucky carnation, was fatally shot at a Buffalo business exposition.

Nine of first twelve U.S. Presidents were southerners

Of the first twelve U.S. Presidents, these men were all from a southern state:

George Washington, Thomas Jefferson, James Madison, James Monroe, Andrew Jackson, William Henry Harrison, John Tyler, James Polk, and Zachary Taylor.

The only Presidents among the first twelve who were from the North were John Adams, John Quincy Adams, and Martin Van Buren.

U.S. has had only one divorced President

Ronald Reagan is the only divorced person ever to serve as President of the United States.

He was divorced from his first wife, movie actress Jane Wyman, in 1949. In 1952, Reagan married another actress, Nancy Davis.

Five other U.S. Presidents married twice, each after their first wives had died. They were John Tyler, Millard Fillmore, Benjamin Harrison, Theodore Roosevelt, and Woodrow Wilson.

Not many made it from mayor to President

Only three men in history who were mayors of American cities or towns ever went on to become President of the United States.

The only ex-mayors to become President were: Andrew Johnson, who was mayor of Greeneville, Tennessee, in 1830 and became President in 1865; Grover Cleveland, who was mayor of Buffalo in 1882 and became President in 1885; and Calvin Coolidge, who was mayor of Northampton, Massachusetts, in 1911 and became President in 1923.

Which U.S. President got the most votes?

Ronald Reagan set a record, which still stands, of getting the most popular votes in any U.S. presidential election.

He received 54,281,858 votes in the 1984 election, the highest total ever.

Reagan also got the most electoral votes in history, 525, in that election.

They carried only one state

The only major-party candidates in U.S. history to lose 49 of the 50 states in a Presidential election were Walter Mondale when he ran against Ronald Reagan in 1984, and George McGovern when he ran against Richard Nixon in 1972.

Mondale carried only his home state of Minnesota.

The only state McGovern carried was Massachusetts.

The next-biggest loser in states was Alf Landon. He carried only Maine and Vermont in 1936 against Franklin Roosevelt, while losing 46 of the then 48 states.

First woman President?

The U.S. once had a woman President for all practical purposes.

It happened in 1919 when President Woodrow Wilson suffered a stroke. His wife Edith took over, deciding what messages got through to the President, and in some cases she made decisions on the affairs of the nation.

Although she was not President in name, Edith Wilson

did, at times, act as President during the last months of Woodrow Wilson's term.

Presidents changed fast

On March 3, 1841, President Martin Van Buren finished his term. On March 4, William Henry Harrison was inaugurated as President. Harrison died a month later, on April 4, and Vice President John Tyler became President.

Within a thirty-two day period three men held the presidency.

Those bearded Presidents

Five U.S. Presidents wore beards on a regular basis while in office.

They were: Abraham Lincoln, Ulysses Grant, Rutherford Hayes, James Garfield, and Benjamin Harrison.

No President since Harrison in 1893 has done so.

George Washington got no popular vote

It's little realized that the general public did not vote for George Washington for U.S. President.

Popular voting for Presidents was virtually nonexistent for the first forty-eight years of the nation's history.

Beside Washington, four other Presidents were also not elected by the public. Those Presidents were John Adams, Thomas Jefferson, James Madison, and James Monroe.

In those days, state legislatures usually chose presidential electors, and average citizens did not have a chance to vote for President.

Slim qualifications for U.S. President

The Constitution gives only three qualifications a person must have to be President of the United States.

He or she must be a natural-born U.S. citizen; he or she must be at least thirty-five years old; and he or she must have lived in the U.S. at least fourteen years.

There's nothing in the Constitution about experience, or character, or anything else.

Theoretically, any person meeting those three ordinary requirements could be President.

Who was the only U.S. Vice President & President not elected to either job?

Gerald Ford is unique in U.S. history. He never ran for U.S. President or Vice President in a national election, yet he served in both positions.

He was appointed Vice President in 1973 to succeed Spiro Agnew, who resigned.

Then, as chance would have it, the President under whom Ford served, Richard Nixon, also resigned, in 1974. Ford automatically became President without ever being elected Vice President or President.

Nixon shares record with Roosevelt

In all the presidential elections in U.S. history, Franklin Roosevelt and Richard Nixon are the only two candidates ever to be elected to the presidency or vice-presidency four times.

Roosevelt was elected President four times, in 1932, 1936, 1940, and 1944.

Nixon was elected Vice President in 1952 and 1956, and he was elected President in 1968 and 1972.

Surprisingly, no one else has ever accomplished that.

Two

U.S. Geography

The southernmost U.S. state

This question about U.S. geography fools a lot of people.

If you ask, "Which U.S. state lies the farthest south?" you'll probably find most people say Florida or California or Texas—but that's not true.

The southernmost U.S. state is Hawaii.

Rhode Island has misleading name

Although the state of Rhode Island is called Rhode Island, it is *not* an island.

Exactly how Rhode Island got its misleading name is not known.

One theory is that navigator Giovanni de Verrazano estimated it was about the size of the island of Rhodes in the Mediterranean Sea, and gave it that name.

Another theory is that the Dutch explorer Adriaen Block called it Roode Eylandt because of its red clay.

U.S. State no longer exists

In 1784, shortly after America became an independent nation, residents of western North Carolina organized a new state. They called it "Franklin," after Benjamin Franklin.

Due to various political battles, the state of Franklin ceased to exist four years later, and what was once the state of Franklin became part of eastern Tennessee.

Native Americans well-represented in state names

Half of all the states in the United States owe their names to American Indian words.

The twenty-five states whose names are thus derived are:

Alabama, Arizona, Arkansas, Connecticut, Idaho, Illinois, Indiana, Iowa, Kansas, Kentucky, Massachusetts, Michigan, Minnesota, Mississippi, Missouri, Nebraska, North & South Dakota, Ohio, Oklahoma, Tennessee, Texas, Utah, Wisconsin, and Wyoming.

U.S.A. doesn't have name of its own

The U.S. is the only major nation in the world that doesn't have a distinctive name to call its own.

The term "United States" is not exclusive because other countries have used that. The official name of Mexico, for example, is the United States of Mexico.

As for "America," all of North and South America share that name.

So, strangely enough, the U.S. really doesn't have a name of its own.

An amazing oddity of U.S. geography

Alaska is both the westernmost *and* the easternmost state in the U.S.

The reason is that part of the Aleutian Islands of Alaska extend so far west, they actually cross the line that divides the Eastern Hemisphere and the Western Hemisphere of the world. Part of Alaska goes into the Eastern Hemisphere.

We don't think of Alaska as an eastern state—but technically it is.

The states with the most and the fewest people

Based on the 1990 census, the five U.S. states that have the most people are, in order, California, New York, Texas, Florida, and Pennsylvania.

It's interesting to note that when the first census was taken in 1790, the most populous state was Virginia. Virginia now ranks No. 12.

The five states with the fewest people are No. 46, Delaware; No. 47, North Dakota; No. 48, Vermont; No. 49, Alaska; and No. 50, Wyoming.

Some people in west Virginia don't live in West Virginia

An oddity of U.S. geography is that parts of Virginia are 95 miles farther west than *West* Virginia.

The state of West Virginia was created in 1863 when citizens there pulled away from Virginia in a Civil War dispute.

That leaves the people living in the part of Virginia that is west of West Virginia in something of a peculiarity. They live in west Virginia (small *w*) but not in West Virginia (capital *W*).

This confusion could have been avoided had West Virginia used the name they almost chose for their state. They were going to call their new state Kanawha, after the Kanawha River. But they settled on West Virginia.

West Virginia was the last state east of the Mississippi River admitted to the Union.

Misconception about Mason-Dixon Line

Contrary to popular opinion, the Mason-Dixon Line was not set up to divide the North from the South.

The reason for the Mason-Dixon Line was to settle a border argument between Pennsylvania and Maryland.

They hired Charles Mason and Jeremiah Dixon to survey the border between the two states. That border became known as the Mason-Dixon Line, but it didn't separate North and South.

Both Pennsylvania and Maryland fought for the North in the Civil War.

Buffalo, N.Y., not named for buffalo

It's a common misconception that the city of Buffalo, N.Y., was named after the buffalo.

The city's name had nothing to do with the animal.

Among the early settlers in the area were the French. They called a nearby river "belle fleuve," or "beautiful river."

The settlement around the river was named Belle Fleuve, which was gradually changed by succeeding non-French people to "Bell-Flo," and eventually "Buffalo."

Could Wisconsin be east of Florida?

Anybody who knows U.S. geography knows Florida is on the East Coast of the United States and Wisconsin is a midwestern state—but even geography experts may be surprised at this:

There are parts of Wisconsin that are east of Florida.

Washington Island, Wisconsin, is farther east than Pensacola, Florida.

Religion percentage of Americans

According to population estimates:

56 percent of all Americans are Protestant
25 percent are Catholic
2 percent are Jewish
2 percent are Moslem
4 percent practice some other religion
11 percent have no religion

Disney parks in different states—but same county

Even though Disneyland and Disney World are in two different states—California and Florida—they are, by coincidence, both located in counties that have the same name.

Disneyland is in Orange County, California.

Disney World is in Orange County, Florida.

Hawaii was Sandwich

The Hawaiian Islands were once called the Sandwich Islands.

They had that name starting in 1778 when they were discovered by Captain James Cook of the British navy. Cook named the islands after the Fourth Earl of Sandwich. Sandwich, at that time, was the first lord of the British admiralty.

Hawaii was called the Sandwich Islands until 1894, when the Republic of Hawaii was established and they took the local name for the islands.

Hawaii became a U.S. territory in 1900, and a U.S. state in 1959.

A city by any other name

Several major U.S. cities originally had different names than they do today:

Atlanta was originally named Marthasville

Miami was Fort Dallas
New York City was New Amsterdam
Boston started out as Shawmut
Cincinnati was Losantville
San Francisco was Yerba Buena

Many U.S. states bigger than entire nations of Europe

Alabama is bigger than Greece ... Indiana is bigger than Austria ... Florida is bigger than England ... West Virginia is bigger than Belgium ... Arkansas is bigger than Hungary ... Maine is bigger than Switzerland ... Kansas is bigger than the Netherlands ... Iowa is bigger than Portugal.

And both Texas and Alaska are each bigger than all those countries put together.

How many states in the U.S.?

Technically, there are really not fifty states in the United States, but only forty-six.

The reason is that four states legally call themselves—not states—but commonwealths.

Those four are Kentucky, Massachusetts, Pennsylvania, and Virginia.

What's the biggest state east of the Mississippi?

All the biggest states in area in the United States are west of the Mississippi River.

In fact, all twenty of the biggest states are west of the Mississippi.

The biggest state east of the Mississippi is Georgia, which ranks 21st in size in the U.S.

Are these places misnamed?

Here are some oddities in American geography:

Virginia City isn't in Virginia; it's in Nevada.

Michigan City is in Indiana.

Then, there's the town of Large, Pennsylvania. It isn't large: population less than 5000.

The Delaware State Forest isn't in Delaware, but in Pennsylvania.

And how about the Mississippi River. It neither starts nor ends in Mississippi. The Mississippi starts in Minnesota and ends in Louisiana.

A "minority" that's not a minority

Although women have fought for equality in opportunities and in treatment as many minorities have, the fact is that females are not a minority in the United States.

According to the 1990 census, there were 127,470,000

females in the U.S. and 121,239,000 males. Females have been the majority in every census since 1950.

Actually, more boys are born each year than girls. Women of all races give birth to about 106 boys for every 100 girls. But there are more females in the total population because women live, on average, longer than males.

Which cost more—a state or a stadium?

The United States originally bought from France the whole state of Louisiana—plus all or parts of twelve other states—for $11 million in the Louisiana Purchase.

But one stadium—the Superdome in Louisiana—cost over $165 million to build—or fifteen times more than it took to buy all those states.

City location surprises

Reno, Nevada, is farther west than Los Angeles, California.

Portland, Maine, is farther south than London, England.

Juneau, Alaska, is farther south than Oslo, Norway.

Pensacola, Florida, is farther west than Detroit, Michigan.

And some parts of Illinois are farther south than Richmond, Virginia.

A most unusual capital city

There's one capital city of a U.S. state that nobody can drive to from within the state.

It's Juneau, the capital of Alaska.

There are no roads into Juneau; it can only be reached by airplane or boat.

Juneau is surrounded on three sides by water, and on the fourth side by a glacier, so there's no way to drive to Juneau, Alaska, from within the state.

More people live in New York City than many European nations

The population of New York City, according to the 1990 census, is 7,322,564.

By contrast, the population of Denmark is 5,134,000; Finland's population is 4,991,000; Norway's is 4,273,000; Switzerland's is 6,783,000; and Ireland's is 3,489,000.

The 7,322,564 New York figure is just for the city proper. If you take the population of the metropolitan area, including New York City, northern New Jersey, southern Connecticut, and Long Island, the figure is 18,087,251.

That gives the metropolitan New York City area more population than such countries as Australia (16,850,000), Belgium (9,921,000), Chile (13,286,000), Greece (10,042,000), Hungary (10,588,000), the Netherlands (15,022,000), and Portugal (10,387,000).

Highest & lowest points only 100 miles apart

The highest and the lowest points in the contiguous United States are both—oddly enough—located in the same county of the U.S.

The highest point is Mount Whitney, in Inyo County, California. Mount Whitney's height is 14,494 feet.

The lowest point is Death Valley, also in Inyo County, California. Death Valley is 282 feet below sea level.

As a matter of fact, those highest and lowest points in all the contiguous United States are just about 100 miles from each other.

U.S. state gets its name to repay a debt

Pennsylvania was originally named "Sylvania"—which means "woods."

But later, to pay off a debt to William Penn, who developed part of the state, the king of England added Penn's name to "Sylvania" to make it Pennsylvania. The king owed Penn money—but rather than giving him money, he named the state in Penn's honor.

Third-biggest U.S. city not a city anymore

The city that was once the third-biggest city in the United States doesn't exist as a city today.

In 1898, Brooklyn, New York, was an independent,

separate city—and as such, was the third biggest in the country, with a population of over a million.

But in 1898, Brooklyn gave up being a distinct city. Brooklyn became merely a part, or a borough, of New York City.

Rochester, N.Y.—the Flour City and the Flower City

Rochester has had two nicknames in its history, which are both pronounced the same but mean two different things.

Rochester was originally nicknamed "the Flour City," because of its flour mills.

Now it's called "the Flower City," because of its annual lilac show.

Portland could have been Boston

In 1844, Asa Lovejoy and Francis Pettygrove settled a new town in Oregon on the Willamette River.

Lovejoy was from Boston, Massachusetts, and Pettygrove was from Portland, Maine. They each wanted to name the new town after their old hometowns.

Unable to come to an agreement, they flipped a coin. Pettygrove won the toss, and that's how Portland, Oregon, got its name.

Juneau the biggest U.S. city?

The largest city in area in the United States is not New York, or Chicago, or Los Angeles, or any city you might think of first.

The largest in area is Juneau, Alaska.

Juneau has over 3000 square miles in its official city limits. By contrast, New York has 298; Chicago, 223; Los Angeles, 464.

Based on official city limit size, Juneau is the biggest city in the U.S. in area.

Eleven of fifty U.S. states named after an actual person

Delaware was named after Lord de La Warr.

Georgia was named for King George II.

Louisiana for King Louis XIV.

Maryland for Queen Maria.

New York for the Duke of York.

Pennsylvania for William Penn.

North and South Carolina were named from the Latin name (Carolus) of King Charles I.

Virginia and West Virginia got their name from Queen Elizabeth, who was known as the Virgin Queen of England.

And, oddly, only one state was named for a U.S. President—Washington.

Which were the last five U.S. states?

It's easy to guess that Hawaii and Alaska were the last two states to be admitted to the Union, but which were the three previous states admitted before Hawaii and Alaska?

In 1907, the U.S. had only 45 states. On November 16 of that year, Oklahoma was admitted.

In 1912, the U.S. enlarged to 48 states with the admission of New Mexico and Arizona.

Alaska was admitted on January 3, 1959, and Hawaii on August 21, 1959.

Two U.S. states have no counties

Instead of counties, Alaska is divided into what are called divisions. There are twenty-five divisions in Alaska.

The other state without counties is Louisiana, where they're called parishes. There are sixty-four parishes in Louisiana.

While it is not surprising that Texas has the most counties (254), it is surprising that Georgia, only the 21st largest state, has the second-most counties (159).

Delaware has the fewest (3).

The county with the largest population is Los Angeles County, with more than 8 million people. The only other county with more than 5 million people is Cook County, Illinois, which includes Chicago, and has a population of 5.2 million.

U.S. almost had the states of Connecticut and New Connecticut

During the Revolutionary War, Vermont changed its name to New Connecticut.

But that name didn't last long. Six months later, in June 1777, they changed the name back to Vermont. The name came from the French words *vert* (green) and *mont* (mountain).

At the same time, Vermont declared itself an independent republic. It remained an independent nation for fourteen years, until admitted as a state of the U.S. in 1791.

These big states don't have much population

Three of the five biggest U.S. states in area rank near the bottom in population.

Alaska is the biggest state in area, but is the second-smallest state in population.

Montana ranks No. 4 in area but 44th in population.

And New Mexico is the fifth biggest state in area, but only the 37th biggest in population.

The exceptions in the top five in area are Texas and California. Texas ranks second in area and third in population; and California is third in area and first in population.

Three rivers run through it

The only U.S. city that has three rivers running through it is Pittsburgh where the Allegheny, Monongahela and Ohio Rivers flow within the city limits. The Allegheny and the Monongahela converge to form the Ohio.

Geographical facts

Of all fifty U.S. states, the most crowded is New Jersey, which has the most people per square mile.

New York City's Park Avenue was originally named Fourth Avenue.

The original name of Los Angeles, California, was El Pueblo de Nuestra Senora la Reina de los Angeles. In Spanish that means the Town of Our Lady, the Queen of the Angels.

The distance across Texas at its widest part is greater than the distance from New York City to Chicago.

There really is a town in America called Hometown. It's Hometown, Illinois, near Chicago.

Three

The Movies

Clark Gable loses the Oscar

Perhaps the biggest upset in the history of the Academy Awards happened in 1939.

Clark Gable had starred in one of the most famous movies of all time, *Gone With the Wind.*

Many people assumed Gable would win the Best Actor award for his memorable performance.

But the award went to a man who's almost forgotten today—Robert Donat, who played in *Goodbye, Mr. Chips*, and Clark Gable never won an Academy Award for *Gone With the Wind.*

What are the odds on this?

By coincidence, four different women whose initials are M.S. won the Academy Award for Best Supporting Actress for four consecutive years:

Maggie Smith, in 1978, for *California Suite*
Meryl Streep, in 1979, for *Kramer vs. Kramer*
Mary Steenburgen, in 1980, for *Melvin and Howard*
Maureen Stapleton, in 1981, for *Reds*

Why Hollywood became the film capital—or did it?

When the movie industry started in the early 1900s, most films were shot around New York City.

Gradually filmmakers shifted to the Los Angeles area because of better year-round weather for outdoor shooting, and because the varied topography offered a wider choice of outdoor settings.

But film companies built their studios in such places as Culver City, Century City, Universal City, and Burbank—not just in Hollywood.

Although the community of Hollywood became the symbol of moviemaking, many studios and film locations—even in Hollywood's heyday—were *not* in Hollywood.

The real Oscar

According to the Academy of Motion Picture Arts and Sciences, the name "Oscar" for its statue was coined by Margaret Herrick, a former executive director of the Academy.

In 1931 she said the statue looked like her Uncle Oscar—actually a man named Oscar Pierce of Texas.

The name "Oscar" for the statue caught on, and it's been called an Oscar ever since.

Why does MGM use that roaring lion?

When Metro-Goldwyn-Mayer was formed, they asked their publicity director, Howard Dietz, to come up with a trademark.

Dietz had gone to Columbia University, whose nickname is "Lions" and whose football song is "Roar, Lion, Roar."

Dietz chose the lion as MGM's trademark, and had that lion roar before each of their movies.

First talk in movies turns out to be prophetic

The first movie in history which had talking in it was *The Jazz Singer*, starring Al Jolson.

The Jazz Singer opened in New York in October 1927.

What were the first words ever spoken in a movie? Al Jolson said, "Wait a minute folks, wait a minute, you ain't heard nothin' yet."

How true.

A famous movie song almost didn't make it

Judy Garland was propelled to superstardom when she sang "Over the Rainbow" in the 1939 movie *The Wizard of Oz*.

If ever a song fit a movie, it was that song in that movie.

But the director of the film, Victor Fleming, wanted to cut "Over the Rainbow" out of the movie.

The men who wrote the song, E.Y. Harburg (lyrics) and Harold Arlen (music), were told by Fleming that the song slowed down the first part of the movie, and it would have to go.

Harburg and Arlen pleaded with Fleming to leave it in, but Fleming was adamant.

Harburg and Arlen then went over Fleming's head to Louis B. Mayer, the studio boss.

Finally, Mayer said, "Let the boys have the damned song. It can't hurt."

Which wife of future U.S. President wins Academy Award?

The first wife of future U.S. President Ronald Reagan won the Academy Award for Best Actress.

Jane Wyman, who was married to Reagan, won the Oscar in 1948 for her role in *Johnny Belinda*.

Wyman and Reagan were divorced the year she won the award.

She gave one of the shortest acceptance speeches in Academy Award history. She had played a deaf mute in the movie, and said in her acceptance speech, "I won this award by keeping my mouth shut, and I think I'll do it again."

Mickey Mouse was Mortimer Mouse

Walt Disney got his idea for Mickey Mouse because he was forced to work in a garage.

Disney couldn't afford an art studio when he started, so he set up shop in an old garage. He was watching mice play there one night, and got the inspiration for Mickey Mouse.

Disney originally called his mouse "Mortimer Mouse," and didn't change it to "Mickey Mouse" till just before he finished the first Mickey Mouse cartoon.

The first public showing of Mickey Mouse was in a 1928 movie short, *Steamboat Willie*.

Which movie won the first Academy Award?

The first movie to win the Academy Award as Best Picture was *Wings*, in 1928.

It was a silent picture (the only silent movie ever to win the Oscar), and it was about air battles in World War I, with spectacular sky scenes.

The movie starred the "It Girl," Clara Bow, along with Buddy Rogers, Richard Arlen, and in a bit part, a very young Gary Cooper.

The first actress and actor to win Best Actress and Best Actor were Janet Gaynor and Emil Jannings.

The Goldfish who influenced Hollywood

Samuel Goldfish came to Hollywood in 1910 and began producing movies.

Eight years later he formed a filmmaking company with Edwin Selwyn. They took the first four letters of Goldfish's name and the last three letters of Selwyn's name and called their company the Goldwyn Company.

Samuel Goldfish liked that name so much he changed his own name to Samuel Goldwyn.

In 1922, Goldwyn effected a three-way merger with the Metro Company and with producer Louis B. Mayer to form one of Hollywood's major studios, Metro-Goldwyn-Mayer. But shortly after, Goldwyn was forced out, and in the many glory years of Metro-Goldwyn-Mayer, Samuel Goldwyn was not involved with the company, although the studio continued to carry his name in theirs.

Goldwyn then became one of the most influential independent producers in movie history for more than forty years, making such landmark films as *Wuthering Heights*, *The Little Foxes*, *Pride of the Yankees*, and *The Best Years of Our Lives*.

Original *Casablanca* was a flop

Although the 1942 movie *Casablanca*, is one of the best-loved movies of all time, the play on which it was based was a flop.

The movie was based on the play *Everybody Comes to Rick's* by Murray Bennett.

The cast of the movie originally was going to star Ronald Reagan and Ann Sheridan, but they were replaced by Humphrey Bogart and Ingrid Bergman.

The song "As Time Goes By," sung by Dooley Wilson, was added to the movie almost as an afterthought.

Consecutive Academy Award winners

Only three movie stars in history have won the Oscar for Best Actor or Best Actress two years in a row.

They were:

Spencer Tracy, who won it for *Captains Courageous* in 1937 and *Boys Town* in 1938.

Luise Rainer, who won it for *The Great Ziegfeld* in 1936 and *The Good Earth* in 1937.

And Katharine Hepburn, who won it for *Guess Who's Coming to Dinner* in 1967 and *The Lion in Winter* in 1968.

The amazing Lillian Gish

No U.S. movie star ever had a longer career than Lillian Gish.

She played in her first film, *An Unseen Enemy*, in 1912 at the age of sixteen. Seventy-five years later, in 1987, she was in *The Whales of August* at the age of ninety-one.

In between, Ms. Gish starred in four of the most famous movies of all time, *The Birth of a Nation*, in 1915; *Intolerance*, in 1916; *Way Down East*, in 1920; and *Orphans of the Storm*, in 1922.

She continued to make movies in the 1930s, *His Double Life*; 1940s, *Commandos Strike at Dawn*, *Duel in the Sun*, and *Portrait of Jennie*; 1950s, *Night of the Hunter*; 1960s, *The Comedians*; and 1970s, *Twin Detectives*.

Her sister Dorothy almost matched Lillian's career. Dorothy Gish was a movie actress from 1912 until her death in the 1960s.

A dog beats humans as top movie star

When the Motion Picture Exhibitors Association voted on the most popular movie star of 1926, they didn't pick a human actor or actress.

Their choice was a dog, Rin Tin Tin. He was one of the biggest box office draws of the silent screen.

Rin Tin Tin was an ex-German army dog. He appeared in his first movie in 1923 and became a star in such 1920s movies as *The Clash of the Wolves*, *Jaws of Steel*, and *A Dog of the Regiment*.

Santa Claus wins Academy Award

A movie actor once won the Academy Award for playing Santa Claus.

It happened in 1947.

Edmund Gwenn played the part of Santa Claus in the movie *Miracle on 34th Street*, and won the Oscar for Best Supporting Actor.

In movie history, actors have won Academy Awards in a variety of roles, but no one would have thought a man could win the Academy Award for playing Santa Claus.

"White Christmas" comes from movie

Irving Berlin wrote the song "White Christmas" for a movie called *Holiday Inn*. It was just one of the holiday songs Berlin wrote for that movie, but it became, by far, the most popular.

Although "White Christmas" is one of the most-sung traditional Christmas songs, it dates only from that 1942 movie.

What's a gaffer?

In most movie credits at the end of a film, you often see the word "gaffer."

The gaffer is the electrician in charge of the lighting

for a movie. He or she sets up the lamps, cables, and other electrical equipment, working under the cinematographer, making sure each scene is properly lighted.

The name "gaffer" comes from the early days of moviemaking, when many scenes were shot outdoors under sunlight. Locations were covered with canvas roofs that could be rolled back or forth to let in the right amount of light. The canvas was moved with gaff hooks used on sails. The person operating them came to be called a gaffer.

Those movie grips

Although many moviegoers have no idea what a grip is, the person known as a grip is usually listed in movie credits.

The grip is a film industry word for stagehand. The grip performs the same duties as a stagehand does in the theater.

The grip literally "grips" chairs, tables, lights, and other scenery and moves them into and out of the scene before and after shooting.

Non-actor wins Academy Award

One man once won the Academy Award as best supporting actor even though he had never made a movie before and had never been an actor.

He was a World War II sailor, Harold Russell, who won the Academy Award for *The Best Years of Our Lives*, in 1946.

Russell had lost both hands in the war and played the part of a disabled ex-serviceman returning home.

He is the only non-professional actor ever to win an Oscar for acting.

Who are Julius, Arthur, & Leonard Marx?

The real first names of the Marx Brothers who made those great 1930s movies, which are still enjoyed, were Julius (Groucho), Arthur (Harpo), and Leonard (Chico).

A fourth brother, Herbert, who used the name Zeppo, left the act in the early 1930s and became his brothers' agent.

Perfect pairing of Bogart and Bergman was a one-time affair

Although Humphrey Bogart and Ingrid Bergman were sensational together in the all-time favorite movie *Casablanca*, they never made another film together during the rest of their careers.

They had plenty of time.

Casablanca was released in 1942.

Bogart made movies for fourteen years after that. His final film was *The Harder They Fall*, in 1956. After *Casablanca*, he was in twenty-eight more movies.

Bergman was active at the same time. She made fifteen more movies between 1942 and 1956—but none with Bogart.

Reagan wasn't the only White House resident to act in movies

Two U.S. First Ladies were once movie actresses in Hollywood.

Nancy Reagan, under her maiden name Nancy Davis, was a featured player in several movies in the 1950s, and she played opposite future President Ronald Reagan in the movie *Hellcats of the Navy* in 1957.

Pat Nixon, wife of President Richard Nixon, appeared in some movies as a bit player in the 1930s. She was in the first full-length movie shot entirely in full-color Technicolor, *Becky Sharp*, in 1935.

U.S. actress helps America's war effort—and hurts career

Veronica Lake was one of the biggest movie stars in Hollywood in the early 1940s.

A main reason for her popularity was her trademark hairstyle—long blond hair that came down over one eye and covered almost half her face.

The problem was that her peekaboo hairstyle began to be copied by women all over America, and women were getting their hair caught in defense-industry machinery.

For the good of the war effort, Lake was asked to change her hairstyle.

She did, and her distinctive look was gone. Her popularity slipped and she quickly faded from movie stardom, winding up as a cocktail waitress in New York.

Movie stars' children win Academy Awards

Five well-known movie stars had children who each won an Academy Award:

Judy Garland's daughter Liza Minnelli won the Best Actress Oscar for *Cabaret*.

Henry Fonda's daughter Jane won for Best Actress in *Coming Home*.

Walter Huston's son John won the Best Director Oscar for *Treasure of Sierra Madre*. Walter Huston also won an Oscar for that movie as Best Supporting Actor.

Kirk Douglas's son Michael won the Best Actor Oscar for *Wall Street*.

And Ryan O'Neal's daughter Tatum won a Best Supporting Actress Oscar for *Paper Moon*.

The first movie

Although the movie process was begun in the late 1800s, films in those days showed only unrelated scenes and moving images.

The first real movie that told a story was made in 1903 and filmed in New Jersey by the director and producer Edwin Porter.

Its title was *The Great Train Robbery*, and moviemakers have had a fascination with trains ever since. Hundreds of subsequent movies have been made with scenes on trains.

A Mrs. Wilcot names Hollywood

The name Hollywood, California, is famous all over the world—but Hollywood got its name in a very ordinary way.

According to the Smithsonian News Service, when Hollywood was first settled in 1887, two people who moved there were Mr. and Mrs. Horace Wilcot.

One day, Mr. Wilcot planted some holly bushes—and Mrs. Wilcot then named the area "Hollywood."

Little could they have known then that the name "Hollywood" would become known just about everywhere.

Movie facts

Citizen Kane, called by many the greatest movie of all time, did not win Best Picture at the Academy Awards the year it was eligible. The film chosen instead was *How Green Was My Valley*.

Alfred Hitchcock never won an Academy Award for directing.

The movie *Oklahoma* was filmed—not in Oklahoma—but in Arizona, because the producers thought Arizona looked more like Oklahoma than Oklahoma did.

Four

U.S. History

Pony Express has surprisingly short life

Although the Pony Express was one of the most famous chapters in U.S. history, it lasted just nineteen months, from April 1860 to October 1861.

It had a glamorous aura, but it was a financial failure and lost over $200,000 in its short run.

Another surprising fact is that despite its name, the Pony Express didn't use ponies. They used full-sized horses—not ponies.

Things you didn't know about Paul Revere

His family name wasn't Revere. His father had come from France and their name was Revoire. They gradually Anglicized it to Revere.

Although Paul Revere is remembered today by most people only for his famous midnight ride in 1775, he was a successful silversmith and engraver. He designed the first American money and made the state seal of Massachusetts, which is still used.

Revere also made fine sterling dishes, some of which are held by collectors and museums today.

He excelled in heavy industry, building the first copper-rolling mill in the U.S., and he manufactured parts for U.S. ships.

On the negative side, Revere was court-martialed for cowardice and insubordination after commanding a failed expedition in the Revolutionary War. He was acquitted, but left the service in disrepute.

Son-in-law and father-in-law presidents of warring nations

The president of the Confederate States during the Civil War was the son-in-law of a U.S. President.

Jefferson Davis, president of the Confederacy, was the son-in-law of the twelfth U.S. President, Zachary Taylor.

Davis married Taylor's daughter Sarah in 1835.

Zachary Taylor became President of the United States in 1849, and his son-in-law, Jefferson Davis, became president of the Confederacy in 1861.

Battle of Bunker Hill fought on different hill

Despite its name, the famous Battle of Bunker Hill in the American Revolutionary War was not fought on Bunker Hill.

Why, then, was it called the Battle of Bunker Hill?

The commander of troops that day had orders to protect Bunker Hill—but he chose to fight the battle on nearby Breed's Hill instead.

The incredible story of Robert Lincoln and three assassinations

One person was on the scene in three different places when three U.S. Presidents were assassinated.

He was Robert Lincoln, son of Abraham Lincoln. First, Robert was with his father after Abraham Lincoln was shot in 1865.

Then in 1881, Robert Lincoln was Secretary of War under President Garfield and was on hand when Garfield was shot at a Washington railroad station.

And in 1901, Robert Lincoln was invited to join President McKinley at an exposition in Buffalo, New York, and arrived just as McKinley was shot.

She was the model for Statue of Liberty

Few Americans know which woman was the model for the Statue of Liberty.

The Statue of Liberty was designed by a French sculptor, Frederic Auguste Bartholdi. While working on the statue, Bartholdi had his mother, Charlotte, stand as the model. He used his mother because he said she looked strong and honest.

Although Charlotte Bartholdi is practically unknown today, her face has been immortalized as one of the most famous in the world.

America could have been named "Vespucci" or "Columbus"

A long-forgotten German mapmaker, Martin Waldsee-muller, was responsible for America being named America.

Waldseemuller was the first to call the New World "America" in an influential map he made in 1507.

He chose "America" from the first name of explorer Amerigo Vespucci, changing "Amerigo" to "America."

Had it not been for Waldseemuller, America might have a different name today. It's conceivable if someone else had made that first influential map, that person might have named the New World after Columbus; or, an entirely different name might have evolved for America.

As a matter of fact, Waldseemuller could have chosen the explorer's last name and called America "Vespucci."

Custer becomes youngest general despite graduating last in class

One of America's most unusual soldiers was General George Custer, the man killed in the famous "Battle of Little Bighorn," or "Custer's Last Stand."

Custer was the youngest general in the history of the United States Army.

He became a general at age twenty-three, even though, just two years earlier, he graduated *last* in his class at West Point!

Ironically, the White House could have been the Red House

If Thomas Jefferson had had his way, the White House would be called the Red House today.

Jefferson wanted it built with red bricks.

The irony is that if Jefferson's plan had prevailed, twentieth century Presidents would have been issuing anti-Communist, anti-red statements from the Red House.

Jefferson's idea of a red brick home for U.S. Presidents was overridden by Irish-born architect James Hoban. Hoban used the home of Ireland's Duke of Leinster as the basis for the design of the White House—without red bricks.

Who wrote the Pledge of Allegiance?

Although millions of Americans have recited the Pledge of Allegiance to the flag, few know where it came from, or who wrote it.

The pledge was written in 1892 by Francis Bellamy, a retired minister. He submitted the pledge to a popular magazine of the day, *Youth's Companion*.

The magazine published the Pledge of Allegiance, and virtually every school in the country adopted it.

You had to be named George to head America

Every head-of-state of America for almost 100 years was named George.

From 1714 to 1776, when America was a British colony, King George I, II, and III ruled America. Then, by coincidence, the first U.S. President was also named George—George Washington. He led America until 1797.

Oddly, after that, there was never another U.S. President named George for almost 200 years, or until 1989, when George Bush became President.

Who were these men?

Here's a favorite question by a history teacher who always marvels that hardly anyone knows the answer.

The question is: "What do these nine men have in common in regards to American history—George Clinton, Daniel Tompkins, Richard Johnson, George Dallas, Hannibal Hamlin, Henry Wilson, Thomas Hendricks, Garrett Hobart, and Charles Dawes?"

Here's what they have in common: They were all Vice Presidents of the United States, but few people today recognize their names.

Many Americans didn't want independence

On the eve of the American Revolutionary War, many Americans were either opposed to fighting the British for independence or were indifferent to the cause.

The majority of the governors of the colonies were also opposed to going to war.

It must be remembered that many Americans at that time had strong ties to England and didn't mind remaining under British rule.

The unique Abigail Adams

Abigail Smith Adams is the only woman in American history who was both the wife and the mother of a U.S. President.

Her husband, John Adams, became the second President of the United States, in 1797.

Her son, John Quincy Adams, became the sixth U.S. President, in 1825.

And her grandson, Charles Adams, was a candidate for the presidency too. In an 1872 presidential convention, Charles Adams led on the first ballot, but then failed to get the nomination.

V.P. indicted for murder

One man continued to serve as Vice President of the U.S. after being indicted for murder.

Aaron Burr, the V.P. under Thomas Jefferson, was indicted for the 1804 killing of Alexander Hamilton in a duel, while Burr was Vice President.

Burr left New Jersey, where the duel was fought, didn't return, and completed his term as Vice President, ending in 1805.

He was never brought to trial on that indictment, but in 1807 Burr was arrested and tried for treason for allegedly attempting to form a republic in the southwest. He was later acquitted of that charge and resumed his law practice in New York in 1812.

Who wrote the Monroe Doctrine?

The Monroe Doctrine wasn't written by James Monroe— the man it was named after.

The Monroe Doctrine was announced in 1823 and became a fundamental policy of the United States, holding that foreign nations had no right to seize any part of North, Central, or South America.

The Monroe Doctrine was written by John Quincy Adams, who was Secretary of State at the time, under President Monroe.

Who would have predicted success for this man?

First, he failed in business. Then, he tried politics.

He ran for his state legislature—and lost.

Then, he ran for the U.S. House of Representatives— and lost.

Then he ran for the U.S. Senate—and lost. He ran for the U.S. Senate again—and again lost.

He was nominated for U.S. Vice President, and lost.

Then, he ran for President of the United States—and won. His name: Abraham Lincoln.

Did Betsy Ross really make the flag?

The legend that Betsy Ross made the first United States flag was first promoted by Mrs. Ross's grandson in 1870, almost 100 years after the alleged event.

There is no clear historical record to back up that claim.

Some historians now believe that the credit should go to a little-remembered Philadelphia judge, Francis Hopkinson.

In addition to being a judge, Hopkinson was an artist. He did design a naval flag, and left a letter saying he made the original design for the U.S. flag.

U.S. population growth

Here's an indication of how America has grown in population.

There are more people in New York City today than there were in the whole country when the U.S. took the first census in 1790.

The U.S. population in 1790 was just 4 million.

Even as late as 1850 there were fewer people in the entire nation than there are in California today (23 million vs. 29 million).

But the biggest growth has occurred since World War II. In 1940, the U.S population was 132 million. It has almost doubled since then to the 1990 total of 248 million.

The first postage stamps

When the U.S. printed the first postage stamps, there were only two kinds. One was a five-cent brown stamp, showing Benjamin Franklin, for letters going less than 300 miles.

The other was a ten-cent blue stamp, showing George Washington, for letters going more than 300 miles.

The White House in Trenton, New Jersey?

The capital of the United States came very close to being Trenton, New Jersey.

When delegates met to choose the permanent U.S. capital, Trenton was the original favorite. But then states started to lobby for the capital to be in their section of the country.

Finally, Washington was selected as a compromise because at the time, it was about halfway between the northern and southern states. But had the vote come sooner, the U.S. capital might have been Trenton.

Patrick Henry was hard to get

Few men in history turned down more big jobs than Patrick Henry.

George Washington wanted Henry to be Chief Justice of the Supreme Court. Henry said no. Then Washington offered to make him Secretary of State. Henry refused.

Later, Henry was appointed U.S. Senator, but declined, and finally, Henry was elected governor of Virginia—but he refused to take office.

Henry turned down all those jobs because he wanted to stay home.

U.S. Vice President never in capital

William King was elected Vice President under President Franklin Pierce in 1852. At the time of the election, King became ill and it was felt that hot sun would help him, so he went to Cuba to recuperate.

An Act of Congress permitted King to take the oath of office in Havana, Cuba. He stayed there for a while, then went home to Alabama, where he died in 1853.

The whole time he was Vice President, he was never in Washington, D.C.

Robert E. Lee could have led the North

There was once a man who was offered the command of *both* sides in a major war.

On the eve of the U.S. Civil War, President Abraham Lincoln offered to make Robert E. Lee the commander of the Union forces. Lee declined even though he was a graduate of the U.S. Military Academy at West Point and had served in the U.S. Army. He told Lincoln that because of his southern roots he could not fight against the South.

Later, of course, Lee took command of the southern forces. He became the only general in history who had his pick of leading either side in a war.

Jefferson failed to note he was President

One of the strangest epitaphs ever written by a man for his own gravestone was the one written by U.S. President Thomas Jefferson.

What Jefferson wanted to appear on his grave was that he was a founder of the University of Virginia and that he had written the Declaration of Independence, among other things.

The one thing Jefferson never mentioned in his epitaph was that he was President of the United States.

Presidential retreat named for little boy

The famous U.S. presidential retreat, Camp David, was named after a young boy.

The retreat was originally built for President Roosevelt during World War II, and he named it Shangri-La.

But when Dwight Eisenhower became President in 1953, he gave the retreat a new name—Camp David.

Dwight Eisenhower named it after his young grandson, David Eisenhower.

Two Abraham Lincolns are murdered

President Abraham Lincoln's grandfather—also named Abraham Lincoln—was also killed by a gunman. He was shot and killed on the Wilderness Trail in 1786.

Ironically, President Lincoln was named after his grandfather—and met the same fate. Also, both Abraham Lincolns had a wife named Mary and a son named Tom.

Liberty Bell had different purpose

The original idea for the Liberty Bell in Philadelphia was not to proclaim liberty for the United States.

The bell was made for the Pennsylvania legislature and was originally used merely to signal meetings for the provincial legislature, starting in 1753.

It wasn't called the Liberty Bell then. Its name was the Province Bell. But that bell just happened to be in the right place at the right time. When it was used to signal the reading of the Declaration of Independence in 1776, it became a national treasure.

The Liberty Bell's famous crack did not occur at the time of the Declaration of Independence, as is popularly believed. It cracked when tolling for the funeral of Chief Justice John Marshall in 1835.

What made the famous Battle of New Orleans so strange?

At dawn on January 8, 1815, the biggest battle in the War of 1812 began as American troops routed the British in the bloody Battle of New Orleans.

But there was something the troops who fought in that battle didn't know.

Fifteen days before, on December 24, 1814, England and America had signed a peace treaty in Ghent, Belgium, ending the war.

There was no instant communication then—no telephone, radio, or telegraph. The troops in New Orleans had no idea a peace treaty had been signed.

They fought that famous Battle of New Orleans *after* the war was over.

Doubleday didn't start baseball—but he helped start Civil War

Contrary to popular opinion, Abner Doubleday did not start baseball—but he did help start the Civil War.

Most historians refute the legend that Doubleday invented baseball. There's too much evidence that shows he had little or nothing to do with baseball.

However, Doubleday was at Fort Sumter, and he fired the first Union gun in the first battle of the Civil War.

Plymouth Rock was not Pilgrims' first landing—and they weren't Pilgrims

When the Pilgrims first landed in America, they didn't land at Plymouth Rock.

The Pilgrims first went ashore in America at Provincetown, Massachusetts, at the tip of Cape Cod. They landed there on November 21, 1620.

The Pilgrims stayed at Provincetown for about a month. Then, in December, they sailed across Cape Cod Bay and landed in Plymouth. There, they found Plymouth Rock and established Plymouth Colony.

The Pilgrims didn't call themselves by that name. They called themselves Separatists. Some 100 years after they arrived, historians started calling them Pilgrims.

U.S.A. had a different name for sixty-seven days

When the Declaration of Independence was adopted on July 4, 1776, the country was called "the United Colonies of America."

Congress waited sixty-seven days to officially change the name of the country.

On September 9, 1776, they passed a law changing the name from "the United Colonies of America" to "the United States of America."

U.S. has had nine capitals

Eight different cities—in addition to Washington, D.C.—have served as the capital of the United States.

Philadelphia was the first U.S. capital, and then Baltimore took over until March 1777.

After that the capital was constantly moved because of fighting in the Revolutionary War. It was located in Lancaster and York, Pennsylvania, Trenton and Princeton, New Jersey, and Annapolis, Maryland.

After the war, New York City became the capital—then Philadelphia again, and finally, in 1800, Washington.

The first telephone numbers

In the early days of telephones, callers simply gave operators the person's name they were calling, and the operator would connect them. There were no telephone numbers.

But in Lowell, Massachusetts, in 1879, there was a measles epidemic, and Dr. Moses Parker, a town physician, felt if Lowell's four telephone operators came down with the illness, telephone communications could be delayed.

Dr. Parker suggested numbers be used for the town's two hundred telephone subscribers so if substitute operators were needed, they could operate the exchange more quickly—and that's when telephone numbers were born.

No iron on *Old Ironsides*

Old Ironsides, one of the most famous ships in U.S. history, did not have iron sides.

It was built with sides of oak. It got its name during the War of 1812.

A sailor is said to have seen a shot from a British gun bounce off the ship's side, and he exclaimed the ship had sides of iron—but it really didn't.

Oliver Wendell Holmes helped popularize the ship with his poem "Old Ironsides."

Washington didn't like Washington's name

George Washington didn't want Washington, D.C., to be named after him.

When the city of Washington was being laid out during George Washington's term as President, he always referred to it—not as Washington—but as "Federal City."

Whether it was modesty or whatever, George Washington never liked the city to be known as "Washington." It was only after his death that "Washington" became the official name for "Federal City."

Pilgrims weren't first

A misconception of American history is that the Pilgrims established the first European settlement in America. That's not true.

A group of Englishmen established a settlement in Jamestown, Virginia, in 1607—and that was thirteen years before the Pilgrims came to America and Plymouth Rock.

And, some historians feel that when the Pilgrims set sail for America, they wanted to go to Virginia, but wound up in Massachusetts only because they were blown off course.

The "what-might-have-beens" for Daniel Webster

You never know when opportunity is yours.

Take the case of Daniel Webster, a U.S. congressman in the nineteenth-century. Webster wanted more than anything else to be President of the United States.

He was offered the vice-presidency by William Henry Harrison, but turned it down. Then Harrison died in office.

Again Webster was offered the vice-presidency, by Zachary Taylor, but declined. Taylor died in office.

Webster never did become President.

A congressman could legally call another Representative "Mother"

In 1952, Oliver Bolton was elected to the U.S. Congress from Ohio's Eleventh District.

That same year, Bolton's mother, Mrs. Frances Bolton, was elected to Congress from Ohio's 22nd District.

Thus, in an unusual footnote of history, a mother and her son were both members of the U.S. House of Representatives at the same time.

Uncle Sam was real

Sam Wilson worked in the food business in Troy, N.Y. He was known as "Uncle Sam" in Troy, and supplied food to American troops in the War of 1812.

Soldiers began saying that Uncle Sam Wilson was feeding the army.

The "U.S." of Uncle Sam Wilson's initials were a nice tie-in, and a legend was born, eventually spreading around the country. Uncle Sam Wilson became the symbol for America.

Who was Horatio Gates?

One of the most underrated heroes of American history is a man you rarely hear of—Horatio Gates, under whose command the colonists won the Battle of Saratoga.

That battle was the turning point of the Revolutionary

War—and some historians call it one of the most decisive battles in the history of the world.

Had Gates lost, the colonists might not have won freedom.

The U.S. really wasn't a democracy

How democratic was the United States from 1776 to the 1920s?

For one thing, more than half of the adults in the U.S. were excluded from voting. Women weren't allowed to vote in national elections until the 19th Amendment to the Constitution was certified 144 years after the Declaration of Independence.

Blacks and others were effectively prohibited from voting by poll taxes and other local laws and customs until well into the twentieth century.

And the public didn't vote for U.S. Senators for the first 137 years of the nation.

No Smith reaches the top

Even though Smith is the most common last name in America, there's never been a U.S. President or Vice President named Smith.

Not only that, there's never been a Chief Justice of the Supreme Court, or a Speaker of the House of Representatives named Smith.

You'd think the odds would have propelled a person named Smith into one of those offices in over 200 years—but it's never happened yet.

Immortal speech got second-billing

The main speaker at Gettysburg the day Abraham Lincoln delivered his immortal Gettysburg Address was not Abraham Lincoln.

The man billed as the main speaker that day was Congressman Edward Everett.

Everett gave the major address, speaking for two hours, and only then did Lincoln get a chance to talk.

Assassin's brother in Hall of Fame

The brother of a man who killed a U.S. President is in the Hall of Fame for Great Americans, which honors great Americans in all fields.

He's Edwin Booth. His brother, John Wilkes Booth, shot Abraham Lincoln.

Edwin Booth was a leading actor of the American theater in the mid-1800s, and was elected to the Hall of Fame for that reason. Ironically, his brother shot President Lincoln in—of all places—a theater.

What freedom of the press?

Although the U.S. Constitution guarantees freedom of the press, the convention at which the Constitution was written, in 1787, was completely closed to the press, and to the public.

And when the Constitution was adopted, it carried no guarantees for freedom of the press, or speech, or religion, or trial by jury, or other freedoms now taken for granted.

None of those freedoms were in the original U.S. Constitution.

Those freedoms were only added as part of the first ten amendments, which were not adopted until 1791.

Critic calls Gettysburg Address "silly, dishwatery"

Of all the speeches ever made, Abraham Lincoln's Gettysburg Address has to rank as one of the most stirring and memorable in history.

Yet, after Lincoln made his speech, the *Chicago Times* gave this review:

"The cheek of every American must tingle with shame as he reads the silly, flat and dishwatery utterances of the man who has to be pointed out to intelligent foreigners as the President of the United States."

As Lincoln might say, "You can't please all of the people all of the time."

Only one American has been both President & Chief Justice

William Howard Taft, who was President of the United States from 1909 to 1913, was the first and only President to also serve as Chief Justice of the U.S. Supreme Court.

Taft had a strong legal background. He had been a state and federal judge before becoming President, and he was a professor of constitutional law at Yale after he was President.

In 1921, President Harding appointed Taft Chief Justice of the Supreme Court, and he remained there until just before his death in 1930.

His son Robert, a U.S. Senator, tried for the presidency several times but failed to get his party's nomination.

U.S. flag had more than thirteen stripes

The U.S. flag once had more stripes than it does now.

When the fourteenth and fifteenth states entered the Union in the 1790s, two stripes were added to the original thirteen, and the flag had fifteen stripes.

However, it became obvious that the flag would be overwhelmed if new stripes were added for each new state.

Congress took away the extra stripes, and said the flag should always have just thirteen stripes.

Mrs. Washington was against independence

If George Washington's mother had had her way, America today would still be under British rule.

Mrs. Mary Ball Washington did not want her son to join the revolution against England.

And Mrs. Washington was so against her son becoming President of the United States, she refused to attend his inauguration.

Were congressmen underpaid?

In the earliest days of Congress, U.S. Senators and members of the House of Representatives were paid just six dollars a day. Furthermore, they were paid only when Congress was in session.

In 1817, they got a raise to eight dollars a day, and that salary lasted until 1856.

Congresswoman makes history two ways

Jeannette Rankin of Montana was the first woman to serve in the U.S. Congress.

She made history in 1917 when she took her seat in the House of Representatives. During her two-year term, Congress voted on whether the United States should fight in World War I, and Rankin was the only Representative to vote no.

Rankin was out of Congress from 1920 to 1940. But Montana voters sent her back to the House in 1940, and as chance would have it, she was there in 1941 when Congress voted on whether the U.S. should enter World War II.

She again voted no. Jeannette Rankin became the only person in Congress to vote against going to war in both World War I and II.

Paul Revere gets lasting fame because of a poem

Another man—in addition to Paul Revere—rode out of Boston to warn that the British were coming on the eve of the Revolutionary War. This man did just as much as Revere but he is not remembered today, as Revere is.

His name was William Dawes.

Revere is remembered because of Longfellow's poem: "Listen, my children, and you shall hear Of the midnight ride of Paul Revere."

But Dawes is a forgotten man in history—mainly because his name didn't rhyme as well as Revere's.

The amazing Sam Houston

No one in American history ever held more high offices than Sam Houston.

He was the governor of not just one state—but two. He was governor of Tennessee from 1827 to 1829, and governor of Texas from 1859 to 1861.

He was also a state legislator, attorney general, and congressman from Tennessee, and then, after moving to Texas, he went back to Congress as a U.S. Senator.

Houston was also a president of a country other than the U.S. He was president of the Republic of Texas for two terms, from 1836 to 1838, and from 1841 to 1844, before Texas became a state.

That's not even his whole career. He led the military forces in the fight for Texas independence against Mexico's Santa Anna. Houston captured Santa Anna in the famous battle of San Jacinto—near what is now the city of Houston.

No democracy in U.S. Constitution

Although the United States government is famous for being a democracy, the word "democracy" appears nowhere in the U.S. Constitution.

The word democracy doesn't appear in the Declaration of Independence either.

And speaking of the Declaration of Independence, you'd never know that was its name by looking at a copy. The word "independence" was left out of the title.

The full title on the top of the original copy reads: "In Congress, July 4, 1776, A Declaration by the Representatives of the United States of America, in General Congress Assembled."

Supreme Court justices don't have to be lawyers

U.S. Supreme Court justices are not required to have any legal training.

That's somewhat hard to believe because those judges rule on some of the most complex legal questions in the nation.

But nowhere in the Constitution does it say that Supreme Court justices have to be lawyers, or have any legal training.

In fact, several justices in the court's history had never attended law school.

And James Byrnes, on the court from 1941 to 1942, had little formal education and never attended college.

"Give me your tired, your poor, Your huddled masses yearning to breathe free"

Not much is remembered today about the person who wrote the emotional poem that is inside the pedestal of the Statue of Liberty.

Emma Lazarus wrote that poem when she was thirty-four years old, in 1883.

Lazarus was born to wealthy parents in New York City and began writing poetry and essays at an early age.

She was also a philanthropist, organizing relief for Jews coming to the U.S. from Russia.

Her poem for the Statue of Liberty was titled "The New Colossus" and gave hope and inspiration to immigrants entering the U.S. The last lines are "Send these, the homeless, tempest-tost to me. I lift my lamp beside the golden door!"

Lazarus died just one year after the statue was dedicated in 1886. She was thirty-eight years old.

Five

Music

Two forgotten sisters wrote "Happy Birthday to You"

Mildred and Patty Hill, two school teachers in Lexington, Kentucky, wrote the music for "Happy Birthday to You" in 1893.

They originally called the song "Good Morning to You" for a classroom greeting. Later, they changed the words and the title to "Happy Birthday to You"—and the song became world famous.

It's possibly the most widely sung song in the world today, but its two creators—Mildred and Patty Hill—are pretty much forgotten.

Surprising omissions in "The Star-Spangled Banner"

If you read, or listen to, all the words in all four stanzas of "The Star-Spangled Banner," you'll find three words missing.

The words "United States" and the word "America"

are never mentioned anywhere in "The Star-Spangled Banner."

Another surprise is that Congress didn't make "The Star-Spangled Banner" the official national anthem of the U.S. until 1931—and that was 117 years after it was written.

Little did Beethoven know

When Ludwig van Beethoven wrote his Fifth Symphony in 1808, he intended the first four notes to signify a knocking at a door. He said it was Fate coming, knocking at the door.

But during World War II those four notes became a rallying cry for the Allies. The first three short notes and then the one longer note sounded like the Morse code for the letter V—three dots and a dash.

The Allies had adopted "V" as the symbol for victory. Beethoven's first four notes from the Fifth Symphony were played every night between programs over the British Broadcasting Corporation, and they were played extensively in the United States and elsewhere throughout the war.

A priest writes famous football song on church organ

The Notre Dame "Victory March"—the song that starts out "Cheer, cheer for old Notre Dame," and is perhaps the best-known football song of all time—was written by Father Michael Shea, in 1909.

One day, at a game that season, Father Shea decided

Notre Dame should have an appropriate song. At the time, they didn't have one.

After the game, Father Shea went to a piano in a nearby building, but someone was using the piano.

Father Shea then went to the Sacred Heart Church on campus and composed the song on the organ at the church. The words were added by his brother, John Shea.

How the Beatles got their name

The Beatles were named by John Lennon.

He was a fan of another group—Buddy Holly and the Crickets. Lennon decided he also wanted an insect name for his group, and he finally settled on beetles.

But he changed the spelling of beetles to Beatles.

The man who wrote "Jingle Bells"

The person who wrote the song "Jingle Bells" had an unusual background.

"Jingle Bells" was written by John Pierpont. He was a clergyman in Boston. The Reverend Pierpont wrote "Jingle Bells" in 1857 when he was seventy-one years old.

His great-grandfather had been a founder of Yale University. And the Reverend Pierpont's grandson was the famous financier John Pierpont Morgan—better known as J. P. Morgan.

The unusual concerto

Maurice Ravel, the highly regarded French composer who wrote such pieces as *Bolero, Daphnis et Chloe,* and *Rapsodie Espagnole,* also wrote a piano concerto titled "Concerto for the Left Hand."

As its name implies, this concerto is played only with the left hand, with the right hand completely inactive.

Some music historians say Ravel wrote the concerto after World War I for a friend who had lost his right arm during the war; but this piece is still played at concerts today by two-handed pianists who use only their left hand while playing it.

"God Bless America" remains unsung for twenty years

Irving Berlin wrote the song "God Bless America" for a show in 1918—but it was never used in that show, and it was never sung in public until 1938.

The song got its public debut when Kate Smith introduced it on a radio program.

Strangely, "God Bless America," which has become one of the most famous songs in the U.S., sat in a drawer—never sung—for twenty years, from the time it was written in 1918, until 1938.

Some music briefs

The English horn is not English and is not a horn. It's an oboe that was developed in France.

Irving Berlin's song "Easter Parade" was originally titled "Smile and Show Your Dimples"—which was a flop. Berlin then put "Easter Parade" words to the melody and it became a hit.

John Howard Payne, who wrote the song "There's No Place Like Home," spent most of his life traveling—and rarely had a home of his own.

The word "piano" is an abbreviation for "pianoforte," which is what pianos were originally called.

Jack Norworth, who wrote the popular baseball song, "Take Me Out to the Ball Game," had never seen a baseball game when he wrote that song in 1908.

Music on phonograph records was an afterthought

When Thomas Edison invented the phonograph, he wasn't thinking of people sitting in their homes listening to recorded music.

What Edison had in mind was a method of storing voice messages. In fact, he called the phonograph a "talking machine."

Music on phonograph records came as an afterthought.

The early deaths of great composers

A surprising number of the world's best-known composers died before the age of forty:

Wolfgang Amadeus Mozart died at age thirty-five.

Frederic Chopin died at thirty-nine.

Felix Mendelssohn at thirty-eight.

Franz Schubert at thirty-one.

George Gershwin at thirty-nine.

Georges Bizet at thirty-six.

"Dixie's" author not a southerner

The famous song of the South—"Dixie"—was written not by a southerner, but by a northerner.

"Dixie" was written by Daniel Emmett, who was born in Ohio. Emmett wrote the song while he lived in New York City.

Emmett wrote "Dixie" in 1859, and although it was northern in origin, it was adopted by the South.

The man who wrote "Taps"

One of the most famous melodies in the world was composed by a man who wrote only one song in his life.

The famous "Taps"—which has been called one of the most hauntingly beautiful melodies ever written—was composed by Daniel Butterfield in July of 1862.

Butterfield was a general in the army before retiring to a career as a businessman.

Despite the success of "Taps," Butterfield never wrote another song after that.

What does "Auld Lang Syne" mean?

Many New Year's Eve revelers belt out the song "Auld Lang Syne" without knowing what that phrase means.

The words were written by Scottish poet Robert Burns, and the music was from an old Scottish folk melody.

It means, in Scottish dialect, "Old Long Since" or "Days Gone By."

It was popularized in America by Guy Lombardo in the 1930s when his orchestra played it on national radio from New York every New Year's Eve. Lombardo later adopted it as his theme song.

Different name for "Star-Spangled Banner"

When Francis Scott Key wrote "The Star-Spangled Banner," he gave it an entirely different name.

Key wrote "The Star-Spangled Banner" in the early morning of September 14, 1814, after watching the bombardment of Fort McHenry in Baltimore.

It was published on handbills the next day with the title: "The Defense of Fort McHenry."

Then, about a month later, on October 19, Key changed its name to "The Star-Spangled Banner."

The story behind "Alice Blue Gown"

Remember the song "Alice Blue Gown"?

That song—and the color "Alice Blue"—were named after an actual person, Alice Roosevelt. She was the daughter of President Theodore Roosevelt.

Alice Roosevelt was married in the White House in 1906. The shade of blue she picked for her wedding party became known then—and ever after—as "Alice Blue."

Those American songs aren't American

"Hail to the Chief"—that stirring song played for U.S. Presidents—is not an American song.

It was written in England by Sir Walter Scott and James Sanderson.

Two other U.S. patriotic songs aren't American either. The tune of "The Star-Spangled Banner" was originally an English drinking song, "To Anacreon in Heaven."

"My Country 'Tis of Thee" is the tune of the British national anthem.

Irving Berlin couldn't read music

One of the ironies of life is that sometimes artists with the best technical abilities can't succeed, while others, without technical skills, became highly successful in their fields.

Irving Berlin, who wrote some of the most popular tunes of all time, such as "White Christmas," "Easter Parade" and "God Bless America," never learned to read music in his life.

Many musicians who can read music never wrote a successful song, but Berlin, who didn't know how to read music, became a great songwriter.

Pardon my back

The only stage performer who almost always shows only his or her back to the audience is a symphony orchestra conductor.

Did anyone ever think of turning a symphony orchestra around and having the conductor face the audience? Since most of the musicians sit somewhat sideways, that might not be a bad idea. You would still see the majority of the musicians—*and* the conductor.

Francis Scott Key was a lawyer—and not a songwriter

The man who wrote "The Star-Spangled Banner" was not a professional songwriter.

Francis Scott Key was trained as a lawyer. He graduated from St. John's College in Annapolis, Maryland, and then practiced law for many years in both Maryland and Washington, D.C.

In the last years of his life, Key was the United States Attorney for the District of Columbia.

He did write a slim volume of poems which were published after his death, and one of those poems was turned into the hymn, "Lord With Glowing Heart I'd Praise Thee."

"Anchors Aweigh" not written for any event at sea

When the stirring U.S. Navy song "Anchors Aweigh" was written, its original purpose was not to celebrate ships sailing away for a famous sea battle or any other naval ceremony.

The song was written by Midshipman Alfred Miles and Lieutenant Charles Zimmerman.

They wrote it for the 1906 Army-Navy football game.

"Rudolph the Red-Nosed Reindeer" didn't start out as a song

The words to "Rudolph the Red-Nosed Reindeer" were written—not for a song—but for a newspaper ad in 1939, by Robert May.

Then, eight years later, Johnny Marks wrote music to those words. Marks and May tried to get someone to record it, but nobody would.

Finally, Gene Autry agreed to put it on the flipside of a record—and to everyone's surprise, "Rudolph" became one of the biggest hits in music history.

The incredible Beethoven

One of the most amazing achievements in the history of the arts was Beethoven's ability to create immortal music even though he often couldn't hear what he was composing.

Beethoven began losing his hearing before he was thirty, and it got progressively worse, until he was totally deaf.

During this period, he wrote many of his most famous works, including the majestic Ninth Symphony.

The composer with two successful careers

Charles Ives was one of the major innovators of twentieth century serious music, and he was one of the great American composers. His Symphony Number Three won the Pulitzer Prize in 1947.

But his illustrious music career was really only a hobby for Ives.

He was a full-time insurance executive in New York City and became wealthy from his insurance business.

The person who wrote "America the Beautiful"

Although many people say "America the Beautiful" should be the U.S. national anthem, few people know who wrote it.

It was written by a woman who was an English teacher at Wellesley College—Katherine Lee Bates.

Bates wrote "America the Beautiful" in 1911 after a visit to Pike's Peak in Colorado, and although the song is famous and well-loved, its author—Katherine Lee Bates—is hardly remembered today.

More music facts

The song "When Irish Eyes Are Smiling" was written by George Graff, who was German, and was never in Ireland in his life.

Likewise, Yip Harburg, who wrote "April in Paris," was never in Paris.

Three musical instruments were named for actual people: the saxophone for Adolphe Sax, the sousaphone for John Philip Sousa, and the spinet piano for Giovanni Spinetti.

When Stephen Foster wrote "Way Down Upon the Swanee River," he misspelled the name of the river. It's the Suwannee. There is no Swanee River in the U.S.

The Woodstock Festival wasn't held in Woodstock, New York, but near Bethel, New York, sixty miles from the town of Woodstock.

The man who named rock and roll

In June 1951, a twenty-nine-year-old disc jockey went on radio station WJW in Cleveland and hosted a program of rhythm and blues songs.

The disc jockey was Alan Freed and he coined the name "rock and roll" for the music.

Disc jockeys elsewhere began imitating his format, and the name rock and roll spread across the country.

The name was solidified when Bill Haley and the Comets recorded the song "Rock Around the Clock" in 1954. It became the first rock and roll best-seller.

In memory of Freed, the Rock and Roll Hall of Fame is in Cleveland.

Six

World Geography
Half the world lives in five countries

Although there are more than a hundred different countries in the world, about half of all the people on earth live in just five countries.

The five most populous countries, which have about fifty percent of the world's population, are China, India, the U.S., Indonesia, and Brazil.

It's surprising to note that Indonesia and Brazil now each have more people than Russia. When the Soviet Union was in existence, it ranked in the top five in population. But with the breakup of the Soviet Union, Russia itself is now the sixth most populous country.

Surprising number of countries end in "A"

An incredible number of countries of the world end in the letter A.

They include: Albania, Algeria, Andorra, Angola, Antigua, Argentina, Australia, Austria, Bolivia, Botswana, Bulgaria.

Cambodia, Canada, China, Colombia, Costa Rica,

Cuba, Dominica, Guinea, Ethiopia, Gambia, Ghana, Grenada, Guatemala, Guyana.

India, Indonesia, Jamaica, Kenya, Korea, Liberia, Libya, Malaysia, Malta, Mauritania, Mongolia, Nicaragua, Nigeria.

Panama, Romania, Russia, Rwanda, Saudi Arabia, Slovakia, Somalia, South Africa, Sri Lanka, Syria, Tanzania, Tonga, Tunisia, Uganda, Venezuela, Zambia ... and the United States of America.

San Juan was Puerto Rico and vice versa

There's an oddity connected with the name of San Juan, Puerto Rico.

The city of San Juan used to be known as Puerto Rico (which means "rich port" in Spanish), while the island of Puerto Rico was originally named San Juan.

As time went on, people began reversing the names, calling the island Puerto Rico and the city San Juan, and that's the way it is today—exactly the opposite of the names they used to have.

Where's the biggest pyramid?

Contrary to popular opinion, the biggest pyramid in the world isn't in Egypt.

It's in Mexico.

The world's biggest pyramid is some sixty miles southeast of Mexico City. Its base covers more than forty acres. By contrast, the largest Egyptian pyramid covers about thirteen acres.

Although the Egyptian pyramids were considered one

of the Seven Wonders of the World, the Mexican pyramid beats them all in size.

Hong Kong is not a city

Many people who visit Hong Kong may not be aware that the name of the city located on Hong Kong island is not Hong Kong. It is Victoria. Victoria is the capital of Hong Kong.

The other major city in Hong Kong is Kowloon, which is on the mainland, across the harbor from Victoria.

Beautiful Taj Mahal built as a tomb

The Taj Mahal in India, which some people consider the most beautiful building on Earth, was built for use as a tomb.

The Taj Mahal was constructed of white marble in 1632, to house the remains of an Indian queen.

The name "Taj Mahal" came about this way: "Taj" means monument and "Mahal" was the name of the woman entombed there.

They liked it so much, they named it twice

Among the cities in the world that use the same word twice in their names are Baden-Baden, Germany; Wagga Wagga, Australia; Pago Pago, American Samoa; and Walla Walla, Washington, in the U.S.

Baden-Baden is in the state of Baden-Wurttemberg, and the city was given its double name to differentiate it from the state.

The name of Walla Walla came from a Nez Perce Indian term meaning "place of many waters."

Wagga Wagga and Pago Pago got their names from local dialects.

Biggest country in the world goes out of business

No major nation in human history ever had its name wiped off the map in so short a time as the Soviet Union.

While it existed, the Soviet Union was the biggest country in the world in size, and one of the most powerful, and yet it lasted only sixty-nine years.

The Soviet Union was created in 1922—and it disbanded in 1991.

Other nations in history have ceased to exist, but no country of the influence and size of the Soviet Union ever lost its name and identity so quickly.

The world's three most unusual flags

The countries that have the most unusual national flags are Cyprus, Libya, and Nepal.

Cyprus is the only nation that puts an outline of its country on its flag.

Libya's flag is the only one that has just one color. It shows just a solid field of green.

And Nepal is the only country that dooesn't use a rectangular flag. Nepal's flag has zigzag edges, almost in the shape of two triangles.

Cold Montreal south of Paris

We think of Montreal, Canada, as a cold-weather city, and Paris, France, as a much warmer-weather city than Montreal, but the fact is that Montreal is south of Paris.

Much of Europe is north of the continental United States and the Canadian cities near the U.S. border.

When flying to London, England, from, say, New York City, it's common to think you're flying due east across the Atlantic, but you are flying very much northeast.

The country with the wrong name

There's one country in the world that many people call by the wrong name.

People refer to the Netherlands as Holland, but Holland is only a part of the Netherlands.

Holland—divided into North Holland and South Holland—makes up only two of the eleven provinces of the Netherlands.

But, oddly, the whole country of the Netherlands is often called Holland, after just those two provinces.

Eiffel Tower was supposed to be torn down

Today the Eiffel Tower is the most famous landmark in Paris, but it wasn't built with that purpose in mind at all.

It was designed by the French engineer Alexandre Gustave Eiffel, who merely meant it to be part of the 1889 World Fair in Paris.

The tower proved so popular that the authorities decided to let it stand, and not to tear it down after the fair.

The little-known big city

Most of the biggest cities in the world are well-known—Tokyo, Mexico City, New York, Moscow, Paris, London—but there's one huge city that doesn't get much world attention.

It's not even the best-known city in its own country.

It has a population of almost 17 million people.

It's located in Brazil, where it takes a back seat in world fame to Rio de Janeiro and the capital, Brasilia.

The city is Sao Paulo.

North America could be West America

In their mind's eye, many people logically picture North America as north of South America.

While that's true, if you take a look at a map, you might be surprised to find North America is also almost entirely west of South America.

Practically the entire continent of South America is considerably east of North America.

Therefore, North America could just as easily have been called West America—and South America could have been called East America.

Greenland isn't green

There's at least one place in the world whose name is completely misleading.

Greenland, near the North Pole, is one of the least green lands on earth. Most of it is covered with ice year-round. It got its name from developers who wanted to encourage people to settle there.

Meanwhile Iceland, which is south of Greenland, has far more green and much less ice. Perhaps Iceland should have been called Greenland, and Greenland should have been called Iceland.

Angel discovers highest waterfall

The highest waterfall in the world is the Angel Falls in Venezuela. Water there drops over 3200 feet, or almost six times the height of the Washington Monument.

The Angel Falls got their name not from any association with their height being close to angels, but from American pilot Jimmy Angel, who discovered them in 1933.

Angel was killed in a plane crash while flying near the falls again in 1937.

Budapest once Pest and Buda

The capital city of Hungary, Budapest, was originally two separate towns, one named Pest and one named Buda.

Buda is on one side of the Danube River, and Pest is on the other side. For years Buda and Pest existed separately.

The towns of Buda and Pest were combined in 1873 to form one city with one name—Budapest.

Languages escape countries of origin

The largest English-speaking city in the world is not in England ... the largest Spanish-speaking city is not in Spain ... the largest Portuguese-speaking city is not in Portugal ... and the second-largest French-speaking city is far from France.

The largest English-speaking city in the world is New York; the largest Spanish-speaking city is Mexico City; the largest Portuguese-speaking city is Sao Paulo, Brazil.

Paris is the largest French-speaking city, but the second largest is Montreal, Canada.

How could you walk from the Atlantic to the Pacific in nine hours?

A man once did walk from the Atlantic Ocean to the Pacific Ocean in nine hours!

The man who did it—Olympic walking champion John Deni—walked across the nation of Panama.

The distance across Panama from the Atlantic to the Pacific is only about forty miles, so Deni was able to walk from the Atlantic to the Pacific Ocean in nine hours.

Nobody has ever built anything bigger than the Great Wall

The biggest thing ever built in human history was the Great Wall of China.

The Great Wall, begun in the third century B.C.,

stretches 1500 miles, averages 22 feet in height, and is up to 32 feet thick.

It's strange that the biggest structure ever built was constructed many centuries ago—before any high-powered building equipment was available—and humans have never built any bigger structure in all the years since then.

Do Eskimos live in igloos?

Contrary to popular opinion, most Eskimos don't live in igloos.

The majority of the world's Eskimos live in shelters constructed of wood, sod, animal skins, or stone.

About the only time Eskimos will build an igloo is when they're traveling.

And they usually consider those igloos only temporary, and not permanent homes.

Many Eskimos have never seen an igloo.

The beautiful blue Danube?

The Danube River, which flows over 1700 miles through Central Europe, originates in the Black Forest of Germany and empties into the Black Sea.

Despite its origination and ending in areas known as "black," it has never been called the Black Danube—but it has been celebrated in song as the "beautiful blue Danube." Alas, it is not always a beautiful blue through much of its course.

If you're in Singapore you're in the city or the country

Singapore is one of the nations of the world whose capital city has the same name as the country.

Others are Andorra, Djibouti, Guatemala, Kuwait, Luxembourg, Mexico, Monaco, Panama, San Marino, and the Vatican.

The Leaning Tower of Pisa goes on and on and on

The amazing thing about the Leaning Tower of Pisa in Italy is not that it leans, but that it's survived all these years, while thousands of other buildings, standing up straight, have come down for one reason or another—while the Leaning Tower of Pisa goes on and on.

How long has the Leaning Tower been leaning? The answer is over 600 years.

The Leaning Tower of Pisa is over 180 feet high and leans over fourteen feet from ground to top. Its lean is caused by ground subsidence, or a settling of the earth around it.

China's unusual time zone

China stretches about 3000 miles from east to west—just about the same distance as from Maine to California.

But although the contiguous United States has four time zones, China has only one.

All of China is on Beijing time. Beijing is in eastern China, which means the farthest western parts of China are also on Beijing time.

When the sun rises at seven A.M. in Beijing, it is still dark in western China for four more hours, or until the equivalent of eleven A.M.

The smallest countries in the world

There are two independent nations that are smaller than Central Park in New York City.

Those two nations, both in Europe, are Vatican City and Monaco. Each is less than one square mile.

The next three smallest countries are Nauru, eight square miles, in the western Pacific Ocean; Tuvalu, ten square miles, the Southwest Pacific; and San Marino, 24 square miles, in Europe.

Countries named after real people

There are, surprisingly, very few nations in the world named after an actual person.

Among the handful of countries that were named after a real person are: Bolivia, for Simon Bolivar; Colombia, for Christopher Columbus; Nicaragua, for Chief Nicarao; Liechtenstein, for Johann von Liechtenstein; Saudi Arabia, for King Saud; and the Philippines, named after King Philip.

The United States of America got its name from Amerigo Vespucci.

A city where fire is practically unknown

There's one major city in the world where there's practically no danger of fire.

It's the capital of Bolivia, La Paz, whose altitude is so high, with so little oxygen, that fires won't stay lit.

La Paz is over 12,000 feet above sea level—the highest capital city in the world.

La Paz went many years without even having a fire department.

Why is it the Dead Sea?

The Dead Sea, in the Middle East, is the saltiest body of water in the world. It is about nine times saltier than most oceans.

It lies more than 1000 feet below sea level and is called the Dead Sea because so little plant and animal life can live in it, owing to its extreme saltiness.

The Dead Sea was first mentioned in the Bible under a different name—the Salt Sea (Genesis 14:3).

The Pacific is really big

Here's a surprising example of how big the Pacific Ocean is.

You could put all the continents of the world into the Pacific—and still have room left over.

The Pacific covers 64 million square miles, while all the land area on earth covers 57 million square miles.

How deep is the ocean? The deepest part of any ocean

in the world is in the Marianna Trench in the western
Pacific, where it's over six miles deep.

Foreign capital named for U.S. President

Which capital of a foreign nation is named after an
American President?

The capital of the African nation of Liberia is
Monrovia—named after the fifth U.S. President, James
Monroe.

Monroe was in office in 1824 when Americans helped
Liberia become a nation. The people of Liberia expressed their thanks by naming their capital after Monroe.

Siberia is cold—and big

The Communists weren't the first to send political pris-
oners to forbidding Siberia. Starting in the 1700s, Russian czars did likewise.

Siberia is surprisingly big. It covers an area one and a
half times more than the continental United States. Siberia has over 4 million square miles and is 4000 miles
from west to east.

Parts of Siberia are colder than the North Pole.

Americans don't have patent on red, white and blue

Although Americans always associate red, white, and blue with the American flag, many other countries also have red, white, and blue flags.

The flags of both England and France are red, white, and blue.

And here are just some of the other countries whose flags are red, white, and blue: Australia, Burma, Chile, Costa Rica, Cuba, the Dominican Republic, Iceland, Laos, Liberia, Luxembourg, the Netherlands, North Korea, Norway, Panama, Russia, Samoa, Taiwan, and Thailand.

Two surprising facts about Canada

Three of Canada's provinces—Ontario, British Columbia, and Quebec—are each bigger than Texas.

And, although Canada is considered a far-north country, some parts of Canada, around Windsor, Ontario, are farther south than some parts of California.

No country has more names than this one

You can call it England.

Or you can call it Britain.

Or Great Britain.

Or the United Kingdom.

Or the U.K.

And if you buy one of their stamps, you won't find any name. England was the first country to issue postage stamps, and they're the only nation today that doesn't use a national name on their stamps. Maybe they don't know what name to use.

This country has two rulers at same time

There's one nation in the world that is ruled by two different chief executives at the same time.

That nation is Andorra, which lies between France and Spain.

Andorra is unique in the world in that it's ruled by both France and Spain. Under laws set up years ago, Andorra is ruled simultaneously by the president of France and a bishop of Spain.

Biggest lake is misnamed

The biggest lake in the world is not called a lake.

The biggest lake is the Caspian Sea, lying between Europe and Asia. It's about 760 miles long and 180 miles wide, on an average.

The Caspian Sea was misnamed many years ago by people who thought it was a sea. But by today's geographical standards, the Caspian Sea doesn't qualify as a sea, despite its name.

Why is the London police force called Scotland Yard?

In the thirteenth century there was a palace in London that was used by kings of Scotland when they visited London. That palace and its grounds were given over to the London police in 1829.

The building and grounds, known as "Scotland Yard," became the headquarters for the police—and the police force itself began to be called "Scotland Yard."

The amazing geography of Indonesia

The nation of Indonesia, which lies southeast of Asia, along the equator, is made up of more than 17,000 separate islands.

And the distance of those islands, from one end of Indonesia to the other, is so great that Indonesia stretches almost as far as the distance between New York and Paris.

One of Indonesia's islands is Java, which is one of the world's most densely populated areas, with 1500 people per square mile.

Fly east for quicker trip

You can fly from New York to London in about seven hours, but it takes about eight hours to fly the same plane on the same route from London to New York.

The reason is a current of air, circling the earth, that

almost always flows west to east. That creates head winds or tail winds which make air traffic slower or faster. If you go east, you'll get a tail wind and go faster. If you fly west, you'll be slowed by head winds.

On longer flights there's even a bigger difference. If you flew around the world, it takes almost five hours longer if you fly westbound instead of eastbound.

Pago Pago isn't pronounced Pago Pago

The South Pacific town of Pago Pago is the capital and chief port of American Samoa.

American Samoa, with its spectacular scenery and South Seas climate, is about 2000 miles southwest of Hawaii. American Samoa is composed of seven islands under United States sovereignty.

The U.S. acquired the islands in 1900 as a naval base. The islands are now classified as a U.S. territory. Residents of American Samoa elect one member to the United States Congress. That member can introduce legislation and vote in committee, but cannot vote on the floor of Congress. American Samoans have free access to the U.S.

The romantic-sounding capital of American Samoa is pronounced Pango Pango.

Two surprises about the Sahara

Most people picture the Sahara Desert as full of sand—but that's not true. Only a small part of the Sahara is sandy. Most of it has a rocky surface with no sand.

The other surprising fact about the Sahara is its size. The Sahara stretches farther than the distance from New

York to California. Its total size is bigger than the continental United States.

Man buys nation—and names it after himself

In 1712, a man named Johann von Liechtenstein bought an area in Europe and created a country—which he named after himself.

That country of Liechtenstein exists today as an independent nation. It is located in the Alps, between Switzerland and Austria. It has a population of about 30,000 and is a constitutional monarchy, still named after its founder, Johann von Liechtenstein.

Everest never climbed Mount Everest

The world's tallest mountain—Mount Everest—was named for George Everest.

Everest was a British surveyor in the early 1800s. He estimated the heights of various mountains.

After he retired, a successor suggested that the highest mountain be named for Everest—even though he didn't discover it and never climbed it.

Italy is a "new" country

We think of Italy as an old country. Its current capital, Rome, was a powerful and influential force in the world going back to 500 B.C. Until the fall of the Roman Empire in A.D. 476, Rome ruled much of Western Europe, the Near East, and North Africa.

But Italy itself was not a unified country until the mid-nineteenth century. It was a patchwork of separate kingdoms, some governed by foreign rulers.

Italy was united for the first time as an independent country in 1861 under King Victor Emmanuel.

Although the Italian civilization is an old one, the nation of Italy is relatively young. In fact, it's younger—as a nation—than the United States.

Where is Casablanca?

In a recent survey, most people could identify "Casablanca" as a famous movie, but many of those same people didn't know exactly where Casablanca is.

Casablanca is the largest city—although not the capital—of Morocco, a nation in northwest Africa.

Before World War II, Morocco was ruled by both the Spanish and the French. It is now an independent kingdom, and its capital is Rabat.

Casablanca, on the Atlantic coast of Morocco, has a population of over 2 million.

The little-known rich nation

The people of Nauru have one of the highest per capita incomes in the world.

Where is Nauru?

It's a little eight-square-mile island in the western Pacific, just south of the equator.

It has a population of only 10,000, and a literacy rate of almost 100 percent.

Phosphate comes from Nauru. The mining and export of their rich deposits yields so much money that the government is able to provide free health care and education for all citizens, and high wages throughout the island.

Oddity of continents' names

The names of almost all the continents in the world end with the same letter they start with.

There's Africa, Asia, Australia, Antarctica, and Europe.

The only exceptions are North and South America, but if you call them just America, that qualifies too.

India named for river that is no longer an Indian river

The nation of India got its name from the Indus River.

But the Indus River no longer flows through much of India. When the Indian subcontinent was divided after World War II, and the nation of Pakistan was created, Pakistan got most of the land surrounding the Indus River.

Thus, today the Indus River is almost all within Pakistan—and not India.

And thousands of miles away, American Indians owe their name to the Indus River, since early explorers of America thought they had arrived in Asia and named local people "Indians."

The five biggest countries in the world

Here are the five biggest countries in the world in area:
1. Russia: 6,592,800 square miles
2. Canada: 3,849,000 square miles
3. China: 3,696,100 square miles
4. United States: 3,618,770 square miles
5. Brazil: 3,286,470 square miles

Three of the top five are in the Americas, with Canada and the U.S. both in North America, and Brazil in South America.

Has any city had more names?

People in St. Petersburg, Russia, have had the name of their city changed three times in this century.

The city was originally called St. Petersburg, named after Peter the Great.

But in 1914, the Russians decided they wanted a more Russian-sounding name for the city, so its name was changed to Petrograd.

Then, in 1924, the government wanted to honor Lenin, and they changed the name of the city again, this time to Leningrad.

But with the collapse of Communism in the 1990s, the name was changed back to St. Petersburg.

How high is Mount Everest—compared to the Rockies and Alps?

The highest of the Colorado Rocky Mountains is just over 14,000 feet—but Mount Everest, in Asia, is more than double that height. Everest is over 29,000 feet high.

The highest of the Alps in Europe is just over 15,000 feet, so Mount Everest is almost twice as high as the highest of the Alps.

Tanzania is combination of two nations—two names

The African nation of Tanzania came into being in 1964 as two countries merged their nations, and names.

One was Zanzibar, which is also known as the Isle of Cloves. It produces much of the world's supply of cloves.

The island nation of Zanzibar joined with the nearby mainland country of Tanganyika, taking "Tan" from Tanganyika and "Zan" from Zanibar plus "ia" from each, to form the word "Tanzania" as the name of their new country.

If every country were like Switzerland ...

There would be no wars in the world if every country were like Switzerland.

Switzerland has not been involved in any foreign war since 1515.

It is unconstitutional for the Swiss government to enter into political alliances or to make war, except in self-defense.

Seven

Money

Which is more: $1000 a day for thirty days, or one penny doubled for a month?

If someone offered you a job for $1000 a day for thirty days ($30,000), or one penny doubled each day for a month, which would you take?

If you took the second offer, you'd wind up with over $5 million.

That seems hard to believe because the second day you'd get just two pennies, the third day just four pennies, and so on—but mathematical progression takes over.

By the tenth day you'd get $5.12. Keep doubling that, and by the fifteenth day you'd be up to $163.84. By the twentieth day, $5,242.88. By the twenty-fifth day, $167,772.16. And by the thirtieth day, $5,368,709.12!

Stock market facts

The lowest figure reached by the Dow Jones Industrial average in the twentieth century was on July 8, 1932, when it stood at 41.22.

The first stock exchange in the United States wasn't

the New York Exchange, but the Philadelphia Stock Exchange, established in 1791.

The American Stock Exchange, until 1953, was called the Curb Exchange, dating to the days when all trading was done outside on curbstones and sidewalks. The exchange didn't move indoors until 1921.

Likewise, the New York Stock Exchange was founded outdoors by brokers meeting under a tree on Wall Street in 1792.

Piggy banks weren't named after pigs

Piggy banks got their name—not from pigs (who were never known for saving money)—but from a type of clay.

That clay was a pliable material called pygg. Pygg clay was originally used to make jars in which people saved money.

Because they were known as pygg jars or pygg banks, they eventually were made in the shape of pigs and later called piggy banks.

Credit cards began by accident

The credit card industry started in 1950 when a lawyer named Frank McNamara finished dinner in a New York restaurant and discovered his money was lost.

That prompted him to conceive the idea for the Diners Club card. That card was originally honored by just a few restaurants in New York City, but the idea caught on.

Soon, other companies got into the act, allowing people to charge many items in addition to food on a plastic card—and a new custom was born.

When the government spends a billion dollars, that's a lot of money

Here's an amazing example of just how much a billion dollars really is.

If you wanted to count a billion dollars—one dollar at a time—it would take you *thirty-two years* if you counted one dollar every second, day and night, day after day, year after year, without stopping.

That's true because thirty-two years is composed of one billion seconds.

Why we use the terms "buck" and "two bits"

A "buck" came to mean a dollar in the early U.S. frontier days when the skin of a male deer, or a buck, brought a dollar on the market.

Also, some of the coins used in the American colonies before the Revolutionary War were Spanish dollars, which could be cut into pieces, or bits, to make change. Since two pieces, or bits, equaled one-fourth of a dollar, the expression "two bits" came into being as a name for 25¢.

If you tear a dollar bill, it can still be good

You can trade in a torn dollar bill for a new one—with one stipulation.

The law says that if you have at least five-eighths of a bill, it can be redeemed for full value.

That may seem like an odd fraction to choose, but if we could trade in one half of a bill, then we could double our money!

The reason it's Wall Street

Here's how Wall Street in New York got its name.

When the Dutch controlled New York City in the seventeenth century, they were expecting an invasion by British forces. The Dutch built a nine-foot-high wall to protect the area where their troops were headquartered.

Later, when the wall was taken down, the street where it had been erected was known then—and forever after—as Wall Street.

Nobody wants this money

There's some perfectly good money nobody seems to want.

Take the two-dollar bill. Several times in history, the U.S. government has made two-dollar bills.

But people don't seem to want them.

The same thing happened in the 1800s with twenty-cent coins. Congress authorized them in 1876, but discontinued them in 1878.

People like money—but not all money.

Man launches oil industry—but doesn't profit

Here's the curious story of Edwin Drake, who drilled the first successful oil well in America.

Drake drilled that well in Titusville, Pennsylvania, in 1859—launching the oil industry.

But Drake didn't realize what he had, and gave up all rights to his well. Then others found more oil, and an oil boom was on.

At the height of the boom, Edwin Drake was a town clerk, filling out papers for people who were making fortunes in the industry he started.

Living person can't be on money or stamps

Here's why no living person can be pictured on U.S. money or stamps.

Originally there was no such law, but in 1864, the head of the Bureau of Currency, Spencer Clark, decided to put his own portrait on a new issue of money.

Congress didn't like this at all, and a law was passed prohibiting any living person's picture from being shown on money or stamps. That prevented any official or politician from taking advantage of that kind of publicity.

Man makes historic deal—and gets fired

Sometimes, you can't win.

Take the case of Peter Minuit—the man who, in 1626,

bought New York City's Manhattan Island from the Indians for trinkets valued at twenty-four dollars.

Minuit's superiors in Holland fired him soon after he made one of the greatest real estate deals of all time.

The reason he was fired was that his personality reportedly conflicted with other colonists and with officials back in Holland.

The property Minuit bought for twenty-four dollars turned out to be worth billions—but instead of getting a reward, all he got was the boot.

Is it really a penny?

Although most people call the one-cent piece a "penny," the word "penny" doesn't appear anywhere on a U.S. one-cent coin.

If you look at a penny, you'll see, on the front, the words "In God We Trust" and "Liberty." On the back are the words "United States of America," "E Pluribus Unum," and "One Cent."

Likewise, on the U.S. nickel, the word "nickel" is never mentioned.

How now Dow?

The Dow Jones stock average is named for Charles Dow and Edward Jones.

Charles Dow was born in Sterling, Connecticut, in 1851, and became a newspaperman, specializing in business news.

In 1882, with two associates, Edward Jones and Charles Bergstresser, he formed the Dow Jones Company. (Although we don't know his motivation, he saved everybody a lot of time and newspaper space by not calling it the Dow Jones Bergstresser Company.)

They distributed business news to brokers, and they founded the *Wall Street Journal*.

Charles Dow also established the first statistical measure of stocks, and that became known as the Dow Jones average.

How checks you write on a bank account got the name of checks

Nobody in the world had a bank checking account, as we know them today, until some 300 years ago.

The first system of writing checks originated in England.

The idea that you had to sign your name on a slip of paper was to "check," or stop, someone else from taking money from your account—and that's why they're called "checks" today.

The man who discovered pearls

One of the world's little-known success stories is that of a Japanese man named Kokichi Mikimoto.

In the early 1900s, he discovered how to make oysters produce perfect pearls. He found that oysters will make valuable pearls if you insert a certain kind of bead under their tissue. Oysters then secrete a substance around the bead that makes the pearl.

The little-known Mikimoto became a millionaire by learning how oysters make pearls—and he launched an industry.

How did the dollar sign originate?

Reference books do not agree on how the dollar sign ($) came into being, but here is the most generally accepted theory:

It was created at first by taking the abbreviation of the United States—the U and the S—and placing one on top of the other.

As time went on, the bottom part of the U was eliminated.

Income tax was illegal

America had no income tax at all for almost the first hundred years of the nation's history.

The first income tax wasn't put into effect until the Civil War, in 1862.

The tax didn't last long, because the Supreme Court declared it unconstitutional. The court cited Article I of the Constitution, which said Congress could levy taxes only with regard to the proportion of population in each state. The income tax didn't become permanent until 1913, when the Sixteenth Amendment was passed. That made it legal for the government to collect income tax for the first time in history.

Unemployment leads to wealth

In Philadelphia in 1929, Charles Darrow lost his job as an engineer.

He found himself with plenty of spare time, so he

spent hours inventing a board game on his kitchen table to keep himself busy.

For the game, he used street names from Atlantic City, New Jersey, where he used to visit.

The name of the game was "Monopoly," which became one of America's most popular games, and Charles Darrow became rich—all because he had lost his job.

U.S. government had more money than it knew what to do with

Congress faced an unusual problem during the administration of Andrew Jackson in 1836.

The government had accumulated a surplus of $37 million, and Congress debated what to do with it.

On June 23 of that year, Congress voted to refund the money to the states in proportion to their representation in Congress.

The next year the panic of 1837 hit the country and revenues decreased. Never again would the federal government have money left over after paying all obligations. The federal deficit started, and it has never been eliminated.

Nickels are misnamed

U.S. coins known as nickels have far more copper in them than nickel. In fact, nickels are made of 75 percent copper and only 25 percent nickel.

Perhaps five-cent pieces should be called "coppers" instead of "nickels."

How would you like to get a paycheck with no withholding tax?

Until 1943, Americans had no federal taxes withheld from their paychecks.

Before that, people were expected to pay their taxes in one lump sum after the tax year was over.

When World War II was in progress, the federal government, faced with the huge costs of financing the war, wanted to get its money sooner. The government then took its tax cut out of people's paychecks, and began requiring quarterly payments or estimates from the self-employed.

After the war, the government didn't go back to the old way of doing things, and that's why we still have taxes withheld from our pay today.

The Dow's fall in the Depression

How far did the Dow Jones industrial average fall during the Great Depression?

On September 3, 1929, the Dow stood at 381.17. Then, on July 8, 1932, at its low, the Dow was at 41.22.

In all, the Dow fell 89 percent in that period.

Eight

World History

King of England couldn't speak English

There was once a king of England who could not speak English.

He was George I, who was born and brought up in Germany and never learned to speak English—even though he became king of England in 1714 and remained king until 1727.

He didn't attend government meetings because he couldn't understand what was being said.

George I left the running of the country to his ministers, and that created the first government cabinet.

Columbus wasn't his name

The explorer whom we now call Christopher Columbus was named Cristoforo Colombo by his parents, and he went by that name for many years.

Later in life, after going to Spain, he changed his name to Cristobal Colon.

He never used the name Christopher Columbus at any time.

World War I had a different name

When World War I was being fought, it couldn't be called that, of course, because nobody knew then about World War II.

During, and after, World War I, it was called the Great War or, simply, the World War.

When World War II started, the first war was renamed World War I. *Time* magazine takes credit for naming World Wars I and II.

Napoleon not French; Hitler not German; Churchill only half British

The famous French general Napoleon was not born in France. He was born in Corsica of Italian parents.

The German dictator Adolf Hitler was not born in Germany, but in Austria, and he didn't move to Germany until he was twenty-four years old.

Winston Churchill, considered by many to personify Great Britain, had a New Yorker for a mother—she was born and raised in Brooklyn!

What if Churchill had retired at sixty-five?

Winston Churchill, who has been acclaimed one of the greatest persons of the twentieth century, would never have achieved greatness had he retired at age sixty-five.

Churchill became prime minister of England in 1940

at the age of sixty-five—and accomplished almost all his great work after that.

Had Churchill retired at sixty-five, the world might be very different today, and Churchill himself would have been just a footnote in history instead of a great leader.

The myth of Magellan

Although you sometimes hear that Ferdinand Magellan was the first person to go around the world, he never did.

Magellan left on his historic voyage from Spain in 1519 with five ships under his command.

He sailed across the Atlantic and around South America, going through what is now called the Strait of Magellan.

Magellan and his ships then crossed the Pacific and got as far as the Philippines. There, on April 27, 1521, Magellan was killed by islanders.

One of his ships completed the round-the-world trip, going from the Philippines back to Spain and arriving there on September 6, 1522, with a crew of eighteen under the command of Juan Sebastian del Cano—but without Magellan.

Women finally get right to vote

The first country in the world to give women the right to vote was New Zealand, in 1893.

Oddly, the next place to give women the vote was the Isle of Man.

The U.S. finally gave women the right to vote in national elections in 1920.

People aged 582 years one night

Many people went to bed in the year 1344, and when they woke up it was 1926—but they were alive and well.

It happened in Turkey. On December 31, 1925, Turkey was going by its old calendar, in which the year was 1344. They replaced the old calendar that night. When Turks went to bed it was 1344, but when they awoke, it was 1926. Everybody grew 582 years older in one night.

Capital of Portugal was not in Portugal

In 1807, the capital of Portugal was moved all the way from Lisbon, Portugal, to Rio de Janeiro, Brazil.

It happened when Portugal was fighting France during the Napoleonic Wars.

The Portuguese royal family moved to Brazil—one of their colonies—and they ruled Portugal from Brazil.

The capital of Portugal remained in Rio de Janeiro from 1807 until 1821.

Some things never change

See if you can guess when the following was written:

"What is happening to our young people? They disrespect their elders, they disobey their parents. They ignore the laws. They have wild notions. Their morals are decaying. What is to become of them?"

You might be surprised to learn it was written by Plato—more than 2000 years ago.

Pianist becomes prime minister

One person in history was both an internationally famous pianist and the prime minister of a major country.

He was Ignacy Paderewski, the pianist who became prime minister of Poland in 1919.

Paderewski made his music debut in 1887 and was acclaimed in Europe and America. During World War I he gave concerts to raise money for Polish war victims.

After the war he was chosen prime minister of Poland, and remained in office almost a year before resuming his music career.

Napoleon never met his waterloo at Waterloo

You always hear that Napoleon was defeated at Waterloo—but that's really not true.

The famous Battle of Waterloo in 1815, at which Napoleon met his final military defeat, wasn't fought in the village of Waterloo.

The fighting took place south of Waterloo, between Mont St. Jean and Belle Alliance, in Belgium.

No wonder it's a wonder

Of the original Seven Wonders of the World, only one stands today—the pyramids of Egypt. To realize what a wonder they are, consider this:

The pyramids were built in approximately 2800 B.C., or over 4000 years ago.

What are the odds against building anything that will last 4000 years?

That alone makes the pyramids of Egypt a wonder of the world.

The world's loudest noise

The biggest explosion in the recorded history of the Earth was not an atom or hydrogen bomb, but an event that happened in 1883.

An eighteen-square-mile volcanic island named Krakatoa in the South Pacific blew up. The explosion was so big that dirt from the island settled in all parts of the world—and the explosion was so loud it could be heard 3000 miles away.

That ranks as the loudest known noise humans have ever heard.

Nero takes a bum rap

One of the biggest bits of wrong information handed down over the years is the famous statement: "Nero fiddled while Rome burned."

When Rome burned and Nero was its ruler in A.D. 64, fiddles hadn't been invented. The first fiddles or violins were not made till the sixteenth century.

And, instead of fiddling, Nero actually led the fight to put out the fire, according to reliable historical accounts.

A family war

Two countries that fought each other fiercely in World War I—England and Germany—were headed by members of the same family.

The king of England during the war, George V, and the ruler of Germany, Kaiser Wilhelm II, were first cousins.

George's father and Wilhelm's mother were brother and sister, and both King George and Kaiser Wilhelm were grandsons of England's Queen Victoria.

Karl Marx didn't know Russia

The founder of Russian Communism, Karl Marx, was never in Russia in his life.

Marx was born in Germany. He moved to France and then England, where he wrote the *Communist Manifesto* and other famous works. He died without ever setting foot in Russia.

The strange story of Lord Cardigan

Lord Cardigan was a general in the British army. He led the famous "Charge of the Light Brigade" in the Crimean War.

He was also the man who popularized a kind of sweater that bears his name today—the cardigan sweater.

But the strange part of Lord Cardigan's story is that he survived many battles in war—then died when he fell off his horse at home.

Taxis take troops to famous battle

One of the strangest military battles in history happened in World War I.

Soldiers arrived to fight the Battle of the Marne—not on foot or by airplane or military vehicle—but in taxi cabs.

France took over all the taxi cabs in Paris to get soldiers to the front.

Victoria in mourning for most of her reign

Victoria was queen of England for over sixty-three years, from 1837 to 1901, but for forty of those years her duties were inhibited by her never-ending mourning for her husband.

Prince Albert, who married Victoria in 1840, died in 1861. Victoria spent the next four decades in mourning, living in virtual seclusion. Only rarely did she appear in public.

Among the few events she attended were those to unveil memorials to her husband.

Victoria spent little time in London, preferring to live in rural estates away from the capital.

The length of her reign can be gauged by the fact that during the years she was queen, the United States had eighteen different Presidents.

The world was sparsely populated

As late as the year 1650, there were fewer people in the entire world than there are in one country—China—today. China today has over one billion people.

The world population in 1650 is estimated at 500 million.

World population didn't reach one billion until the early 1800s.

The rate of population has increased dramatically since then. It grew to 2.5 billion in 1950; to 4.4 billion by 1980; and 5.4 billion by 1990.

It took thousands of years for the world population to reach its first billion, but recently it has taken only ten years to increase by a billion.

The legacy of Florence Nightingale

Florence Nightingale was from a wealthy English family, but she was born in Florence, Italy, in 1820, where her parents happened to be at the time. They named her Florence after the city of her birth.

In her early twenties she took up the cause of hospital care for soldiers in England and other countries. She was appalled at the lack of sanitation and the lack of training of nurses.

She devoted her life to improving hospital conditions, and was the founder of modern nursing, making it a respected profession.

Nightingale is famous for her work during the Crimean War in the 1850s, and England honored her as the first woman ever to receive the Order of Merit.

For 183 years, it was King Louis in France

From 1610 until the French Revolution in 1793, every king of France was named Louis—and they were an interesting bunch.

Louis XIII ruled from 1610 until 1643 and was influenced by his famous minister, Cardinal Richelieu. Louis was only nine years old when he ascended to the throne, and was forced into a marriage at age fourteen. He died at age forty-two.

His son, Louis XIV, became one of the longest ruling monarchs in history, reigning over France for seventy-two years, from 1643 until 1715. He said, "I am the State."

Louis XV, king from 1715 to 1774, became famous for saying, "After me, the deluge." His mistresses included Mme. Pompadour and Mme. Du Barry.

Louis XVI, king until he was beheaded in 1793 during the Revolution, was married to the notorious Marie Antoinette.

Here's one famous explorer who wasn't a hero to some who knew him

The Hudson River is the largest river in New York State, and Hudson Bay is an enormous inland sea in Canada. Both the Hudson River and Hudson Bay were named after Henry Hudson.

Hudson was an English explorer with a reputation for courage. He made four voyages to the New World, sailing up what is now the Hudson River and, on his final trip, negotiating the ice-clogged waters of what is now Hudson Bay.

But Hudson was destined to meet an inglorious death.

After spending a miserable winter around Hudson Bay in 1610-11, some members of Hudson's crew captured this famous explorer and set him adrift in a small boat, leaving him to die of starvation and the freezing cold.

Churchill's strange superstition came true

Winston Churchill, prime minister of England during World War II, lived with an odd superstitious fear for most of his life.

Churchill went through life fearing each year that he would die on January 24 because his father had died on that date in 1895.

On January 24, 1965, Winston Churchill did indeed pass away—seventy years to the day his father died.

Peace prize honors inventor of dynamite

Oddly, the Nobel Peace Prize is named after the man who invented dynamite and new kinds of gunpowder.

The Nobel Prizes are named for Alfred Nobel, who invented dynamite in 1867 and various kinds of gunpowder in the 1880s.

Nobel left $9 million, the interest on which is given to each year's Nobel Prize winners.

So, ironically, the Nobel Peace Prize honors the man who gave the world new explosives.

England gets a twenty-four-year-old prime minister

England once elected a prime minister who was just twenty-four years old.

This unusual man was William Pitt. He entered Parliament in 1781, at age twenty-two, and his first speech impressed the nation. Two years later he was elected prime minister.

William Pitt was the youngest elected political leader of a major nation in history.

The shortest war

There was once a war between two nations that lasted thirty-eight minutes.

That stands as the shortest war in history between nations.

The war was between England and Zanzibar. England attacked Zanzibar at 9:02 A.M. on August 27, 1896, and Zanzibar surrendered at 9:40 A.M.—thirty-eight minutes after the war started.

You never know how a person will turn out

Albert Einstein did poorly in elementary school, and he failed his first college entrance exam at Zurich Polytechnic. But he became one of the greatest scientists in the history of the world.

Winston Churchill stuttered as a child, yet became one of the most powerful speakers ever known.

Napoleon finished near the bottom of his class at military school, yet became one of the leading military men of all time.

Russia controlled Alaska for 126 years

In 1741, the czar of Russia hired Danish sea captain Vitus Bering to explore the waters around Alaska. Russia then took control of all of Alaska.

By the 1860s, however, Russia started losing interest in Alaska because the valuable fur trading it gave them began to diminish. The Russians killed so many fur-bearing animals that those few left made fur trading increasingly less profitable.

The Russians were eager to sell Alaska, and the United States bought it for about two cents an acre in 1867.

The sale was ridiculed by many Americans who called it "Seward's Folly," after Secretary of State William Seward, who arranged the purchase.

But it turned out to be one of the great bargains in history—and removed Russia from the North American continent.

Two wars have deceiving names

Two famous wars in history have names that are not quite accurate.

One is the French and Indian War, fought in America. The other is the Hundred Years War in Europe.

Despite its name, the French and Indian War wasn't between the French and the Indians, but between the

French and the British. The Indians fought with the French.

And the Hundred Years War lasted not just 100 years, but 116 years, from 1337 to 1453.

That really wasn't King George

King George VI, who was king of England during World War II, was really not King George.

His name was Albert. But when he unexpectedly became king upon King Edward's abdication, he bowed to Queen Victoria's dying wish that no one would ever be called "King Albert."

Victoria's husband was named Albert, and she had requested no future king use that name.

When Albert became king in 1936, he changed his name to George and was known as King George.

Panama Canal almost the Nicaragua Canal— but a stamp changes that

In 1904, there was a debate in the U.S. Congress over whether to build a canal in Nicaragua or Panama. Opponents of Nicaragua showed members of Congress a Nicaraguan stamp. That stamp pictured a volcano in Nicaragua.

Congress was afraid the volcano in Nicaragua might someday destroy the canal.

So, Congress voted instead to build the canal in Panama—all because of a postage stamp.

The odd story of Napoleon and the islands

Although Napoleon gained his fame on the mainland of Europe, he was born on an island (Corsica, in the Mediterranean Sea) . . . he was exiled to an island (Elba, in the Gulf of Follonica) . . . and he died on an island (St. Helena, in the Atlantic Ocean).

Not only that, but the woman Napoleon married, Josephine, was from an island—Martinique, in the Caribbean.

Experts can be wrong too

Here is a sampling of experts who have been dead wrong in the course of history:

Scientists once said the laws of physics would never allow airplanes to fly.

Industrialists said telephones were playthings and had no commercial value.

Bankers said before the Great Depression that there would be no depression.

An astronomer said in 1932 there was no hope of humans ever reaching the moon because it would be impossible to escape the Earth's gravity.

England's prime minister said there would be "peace in our time" right before World War II.

Professional pollsters said Thomas Dewey would easily beat Harry Truman for the U.S. presidency in 1948.

Little England a mighty force

England was once the mightiest nation in the world, even though their homeland occupies less than one percent of the Earth's land area.

From that incredibly small speck of land, England spread its language and influence to such farflung places as Australia, America, Africa, Asia, and many places in between, and controlled the largest empire in history.

The amazing Louis Braille

It's hard to believe that the world-famous Braille system of reading for the blind was invented by a teenager.

But Louis Braille of France developed that system in 1824 when he was just fifteen years old.

Braille, himself, became blind at age three. He got through school by forcing himself to memorize what his teachers said.

However, he felt that blind children in the future should not have to do that. Before his sixteenth birthday he had created the Braille system of reading.

Do humans own the Earth?

The insignificance of humans in relation to the history of the Earth can be seen in this fact:

Humans have been on Earth *less* than two percent of the time in the planet's existence.

The Earth existed billions of years without humans.

There are many forms of life that have lived on the

Earth longer than human beings, and there are many other species that had a longer stay on the Earth than humans have.

Flags don't stay the same

Almost every major nation in the world has changed its flag over the years.

Russia's white, blue, and red-striped flag was replaced by the hammer and sickle after World War I. Then Russia changed back to its old flag in the 1990s.

Canada didn't adopt its maple leaf flag until 1965.

France's famous tricolor dates only from the French Revolution of the late 1700s.

England changed its flag, adding the crosses of Scotland and Ireland, in 1801.

China's present flag of yellow stars on a red background was adopted after the Communists took power in 1949.

The United States flag has been changed twenty-six times, with new stars or groups of stars added when new states entered the Union.

The oldest national flag in the world is Denmark's, which has remained unchanged since the thirteenth century.

Nine

Travel

Big airport named for man who shot down airplanes

One of America's major airports—Chicago's O'Hare Field—was named after a man who shot down airplanes.

O'Hare Field was named for Edward O'Hare. In a famous battle in the Pacific in World War II, O'Hare was flying his plane when he found himself alone in the air as six enemy aircraft appeared.

He shot down all six, one at a time, and became a hero.

After the war, Chicago named its airport for O'Hare.

The first freeways

The first of the modern automobile freeways or superhighways—with multiple lanes in each direction and no traffic lights—was built by Italy in 1924. It was called the "autostrada."

The next country to build one was Germany in the mid-1930s, when they constructed their autobahn.

Modern superhighways came to the U.S. in 1940 with the opening of the Pennsylvania Turnpike and the first

California freeway, connecting Los Angeles and Pasadena.

Inventor of airplane didn't like to fly

Orville Wright, one of the inventors of the airplane, never traveled by airplane the last thirty-three years of his life.

Wright had a nerve injury that caused him discomfort when he flew, so from 1915 till he died in 1948, Wright never stepped inside an airplane.

Hertz made yellow cabs yellow

Taxicabs in most cities are painted yellow because of John D. Hertz.

Hertz—who became better known for starting a rental-car company in 1924—also owned a taxicab company in Chicago. He had a study made by the University of Chicago to determine what color was the easiest to see from far away.

The University of Chicago said it was yellow, so Hertz painted his taxicabs yellow—and started that tradition nationwide.

In how many countries do you drive on the left?

Although people in the majority of countries of the world drive on the right side of roads, there are some fifty nations in which people drive on the left.

People drive on the left in England and many of the former English colonies such as Australia and New Zealand—but not the U.S. or Canada.

There are also several nations that are not former English possessions but where people nonetheless drive on the left side of roads. Among those nations are Japan and Finland.

First airline service—without airplanes

The first scheduled airline service in the world began—without airplanes.

That first airline company was organized in 1910 in Germany by Count Ferdinand von Zeppelin. They used—instead of airplanes—a fleet of blimp-type airships called dirigibles. Those dirigibles were also sometimes called zeppelins, after the founder of the company.

Dirigibles carried passengers on routes within Germany, and eventually around the world.

The use of dirigibles for regular airline passenger service ended with the explosion of the Hindenburg in 1937.

First U.S. air service

The first regularly scheduled airplane passenger service in the United States was between—not New York or Washington or Chicago or Los Angeles—but Tampa and St. Petersburg, Florida.

America's first commercial airline, making regular passenger flights, was started by a man named Tony Jannus, in 1914.

He ran regular flights twenty-five miles across Tampa Bay, linking the cities of Tampa and St. Petersburg—and that was the beginning of the U.S. airline industry.

Those automobiles were named for real people

Buicks were named for David Buick. He was originally a plumber. Later he formed the Buick auto company, went broke, and wound up as a clerk in a Detroit trade school.

Chryslers were named for Walter Chrysler. He was once president of the Buick Motor Company, but later founded the Chrysler Company.

Oldsmobiles were named for Ransom E. Olds, whose initials were used on REO trucks.

Dodges were named for two brothers, John and Horace Dodge.

The Rolls-Royce was named for two British engineers, Charles Rolls and Henry Royce.

The Mercedes Benz was half named for Karl Benz, a German engineer. Mercedes was the name of the daughter of his partner, Gottlieb Daimler.

Chevrolets were named for Louis Chevrolet. After his death in 1941, as legend has it, friends asked his widow what kind of car she was driving, and she said, "a Dodge."

World's worst airplane crash doesn't happen in the air

On March 27, 1977, two jumbo jets, a Pan Am 747 and a KLM 747, were on a runway in Tenerife, Canary Islands.

They ran into each other, killing 582 people.

That was the worst airplane crash in the first seventy-five years of aviation, and the irony is that it happened— not in the air—but on the ground.

The man who created yellow school buses

The reason school buses are bright yellow is because of a man named Frank Cyr.

In 1939, Cyr was a rural education expert at Columbia Teachers College in New York. He knew youngsters throughout the nation were being carried to school in an odd assortment of buses of all colors.

Cyr recommended a high-visibility color for safety, now known as "school bus yellow"—and he is the "father of the yellow school bus."

Langley invented the airplane too

A forgotten man of history is Samuel Langley, who could easily be remembered as the father of the airplane, instead of the Wright brothers.

Langley built an airplane before the Wright Brothers, but the Wrights got theirs in the air first. Langley's plane was later flown, proving it was successful, and his theories on flying were used by the Wright brothers.

But because the Wright brothers beat Langley by the smallest of margins, Samuel Langley missed everlasting fame.

Why do we use red and green traffic lights?

Why do red traffic lights mean "stop" and green traffic lights mean "go"?

Why those two particular colors?

It started by chance. Long before automobiles were invented, the first traffic signals for trains in England just happened to be red for stop and green for go.

Years later, when electric traffic signals for autos began, people in England, and elsewhere, continued to use those colors—and the tradition was born.

Coffee, tea, and milk served by nurses in the air

The first flight attendants were a group of nurses organized by Ellen Church, for United Airlines, in 1930.

The safety and well-being of passengers was of such major concern in the early days of commercial aviation, it was felt that nurses would make the best flight attendants.

Other airlines copied United's idea at first, but gradually non-nurses took over the job.

The first auto license plates

The first state to require license plates for automobiles was New York, in 1901—but instead of issuing plates like today, they made car owners display their own initials on the cars—and all owners had to make their own license plates.

Soon other states required plates, but only after several years did the states themselves make the plates and issue them to auto owners.

Parachutes invented before airplanes

Surprisingly, the parachute was invented more than a hundred years before the airplane.

The world's first successful parachute jump was made in 1787.

The jumper was Jacques Gernerin of France.

He parachuted some 3000 feet from a hot air balloon.

Why are they called "limousines"?

Limousines got their name because they were first built in the Limousin region of France.

The biggest limo ever built was 100 feet long, with 26 wheels. It has been used in movies and exhibitions.

The biggest airplane ever built

The world's biggest airplane wasn't built in recent years, but in the 1940s.

It was called the Spruce Goose. It was made of wood—but that wood wasn't spruce. It was birch.

The plane was conceived by industrialist Howard Hughes to ferry soldiers and tanks.

It had a wing span of over 300 feet, or longer than a football field.

Its length was over 200 feet.

The Spruce Goose flew only once, with Hughes at the controls.

Why does Chicago's O'Hare Airport have symbol of ORD?

The original name of O'Hare Field was Orchard Park, before it was changed to O'Hare.

When three-letter codes were assigned to all major airports, they chose the letters ORD from three letters in the word "orchard."

Hardly anybody paid attention to first airplane flight

When the Wright brothers made the first successful airplane flight in history, at Kitty Hawk, North Carolina, on December 17, 1903, most newspapers in the United States didn't even mention it.

Contrast that with the first space flights, at which newspapers, along with radio and TV, devoted complete coverage.

The most significant flight ever—the very first airplane flight—was, strangely enough, hardly reported at all.

The story of the first parking meters

The first parking meters in the world were installed on July 16, 1935, in Oklahoma City.

The parking meter was the invention of Carl Magee, a member of the Oklahoma City traffic committee.

At first many motorists parked by the meters on purpose—just to see how they worked.

And by coincidence, the name of that street on which the first parking meters in the world were placed, was Park Avenue.

It's easier to say KLM

The initials KLM in the name of the Dutch airline stand for Koninklijke-Luchtvaart-Maatschappij.

KLM, founded in 1919, is the oldest airline operating in the world today.

The official name of the company is KLM Royal Dutch Airlines, and its headquarters is in Amsterdam, Netherlands.

Lindbergh not the first to fly Atlantic

Contrary to popular opinion, Charles Lindbergh was *not* the first person to fly across the Atlantic Ocean.

Lindbergh became world famous in 1927 because he was the first to fly the Atlantic alone—but 78 other people flew the Atlantic before Lindbergh.

The first airplane flight across the Atlantic was in 1919—eight years before Lindbergh—by Albert Read and a crew of five.

Ten

Art, Architecture, Books, Drama

Whistler's mother a substitute

One of the world's best-known paintings—*Whistler's Mother*—was painted by accident.

James Whistler had an appointment to paint a portrait one day, but the person to be painted failed to show.

Whistler then asked his mother, Anne Whistler, to pose for him—and her portrait became a classic.

By the way, Whistler originally called the portrait "An Arrangement in Black and Grey." Only later did this famous painting get its other name, *Whistler's Mother*.

Young woman creates Frankenstein

Frankenstein was written by a twenty-year-old woman.

Mary Godwin Shelley wrote the horror story in 1818. At the time, she was the twenty-year-old wife of poet Percy Shelley.

A popular misconception is that "Frankenstein" was the name of the monster. But in the story, it's the person who made the monster who is named Frankenstein. The monster itself had no name.

Theater facts

The action in Shakespeare's *A Midsummer Night's Dream* takes place—not in midsummer—but in spring.

In the plays *Harvey, Bernardine*, and *Edward, My Son*, the character named in the title never appears on stage.

The shortest run any professional play ever had was the *Intimate Review* in London in 1930. Not only did it close after opening night, but parts of it were eliminated during its one showing, so it actually lasted less than one performance.

The merchant in Shakespeare's *Merchant of Venice* is not Shylock, as many believe, but Antonio.

White House wasn't white

The White House in Washington originally wasn't white—and it wasn't called the "White House."

It was gray when built, and was called the "Executive Mansion."

But it was burned by the British during the War of 1812, and to cover up the burn marks, the house was painted white. That's how the White House became white.

The name "White House" wasn't used officially until Theodore Roosevelt was President in the early 1900s.

U.S. gets Smithsonian in strange way

One of the strangest gifts the United States ever received resulted in a famous institution.

An Englishman, James Smithson, gave his fortune to the U.S. to establish the Smithsonian Institution.

What made the gift strange—and unexpected—was that Smithson had no ties with America and had never been in America in his life. But he was angry at the British establishment for what he thought was a lack of respect. In retaliation, he left his money to the U.S.—and as result, Washington, D.C., has the Smithsonian Institution today.

Popular painting has many errors

In the famous painting *Washington Crossing the Delaware* there are major factual errors.

The painting is supposed to show Washington crossing the Delaware in 1776, yet the flag shown in the picture is one that was not used till 1777.

In addition, the type of boat is wrong, the weather is wrong, the time of day is wrong, and the uniforms on the men are wrong.

Despite the errors, the picture became one of the most popular in America.

Gone With the Wind facts

Margaret Mitchell, who wrote one of the world's most successful books, *Gone With the Wind*, never wrote a book before that, and never wrote another book after that.

Also, it's not generally known that Miss Mitchell had a different title for *Gone With the Wind*. She called it "Tomorrow Is Another Day," but her publisher changed it to *Gone With the Wind*.

The publisher also changed the heroine's name from Pansy O'Hara to Scarlett O'Hara.

How the Pentagon got its name and shape

When architects drew plans for the Pentagon, in 1941, the property where the building was to be erected was cut off at one corner by an existing road.

That led the designers to propose a pentagonal, or five-sided, structure.

Then it was decided to name the building after its shape—so, it was called the Pentagon.

The man who drew Santa Claus

A nineteenth century political cartoonist, Thomas Nast, created three of the most famous drawings in history.

Nast invented the donkey for the Democratic Party and the elephant for the Republicans. And Nast was the person who created the modern version of Santa Claus.

It was Nast who gave Santa his familiar red suit and beard.

Nast was born in Germany, came to America, and is credited with developing political cartooning—in addition to Santa Claus.

Shakespeare was panned

Even William Shakespeare was not spared criticism of his writing.

The novelist Leo Tolstoy once said of Shakespeare: "His works have nothing in common with art or poetry."

The writer Voltaire described some of Shakespeare's plays as bad.

And, through the years, there have been recurring theories that Shakespeare, given his limited educational background and lack of travel abroad, could not possibly have written much of the work attributed to him.

If Van Gogh were only alive today

Life is full of ironies, but it's hard to top what happened to Vincent Van Gogh.

Van Gogh made more than fifteen hundred paintings, but he was able to sell only *one* of them in his lifetime, *The Red Vineyard*. It's believed he got only about thirty dollars for the one painting he sold.

After his death, of course, many of his paintings sold at astronomical prices.

Van Gogh should have been a millionaire, but he lived in poverty because his paintings weren't appreciated until after he died.

Amateur designs Capitol building

Although the U.S. Capitol building is one of the most beautiful buildings in America, it was originally designed—not by a professional architect—but by an amateur.

Congress established a contest for someone to design the Capitol in 1793, and the winner was Dr. William Thornton, who had no training as an architect. He was awarded $500 and a city lot.

Is it a Webster's dictionary?

Any dictionary can be called a "Webster's dictionary."

Noah Webster published the first major dictionary in the U.S. in the early 1800s. He, by the way, was no relation to the more famous Daniel Webster.

But Noah Webster's rights to dictionaries ran out a long time ago, and the word "Webster's" for a dictionary has entered the public domain.

That means any company can call its dictionaries "Webster's"—and many companies do.

War author never saw war

One of the most famous books written about war was Stephen Crane's Civil War book, *The Red Badge of Courage*. It has been praised as great writing because of its realism and vivid descriptions of war, but the fact is, when Stephen Crane wrote the book, he had never been in war himself, and had never seen a battle in his life.

How did Venus de Milo get its name?

One of the most famous statues in the world—the Venus de Milo—was unearthed by accident.

A Greek farmer was digging in his field one day and found an ancient statue of Venus, the goddess of love. The statue, with both arms missing, was purchased from the farmer by a French ambassador and given to French King Louis XVIII in 1820.

Because it had been unearthed on the Greek island of Milos, Louis gave it the name of Venus of Milos, or Venus de Milo, and he presented it to the Louvre Museum in Paris, where it remains a major attraction.

In which state was Tennessee Williams born?

American playwright Tennessee Williams was not born in Tennessee.

He was born Thomas Lanier Williams in Columbus, Mississippi, in 1914.

He grew up in Mississippi and in St. Louis, Missouri, and attended the University of Iowa.

Although he had no lifetime experience in Tennessee, Williams changed his first name in honor of his East Tennessee ancestors.

The most valuable painting

Leonardo da Vinci's *Mona Lisa*, which measures only a little more than twenty inches across and thirty inches down, was assessed for insurance purposes many years ago at $100 million.

If it were ever sold, it's likely it would bring a higher price.

Legend has it that the man it was painted for, Francesco Del Giocondo, the husband of the woman in the painting, disliked the painting and refused it. You might say Francesco Del Giocondo was not an astute art collector.

Washington Monument benefits from lack of funds

Sometimes, bad luck is really good luck. Take the case of the Washington Monument in Washington, D.C.

Originally, the Washington Monument was to be surrounded by a 100-foot-high round building.

But organizers had trouble raising money, and cursing their bad luck, scrapped plans for the round building at the base of the monument.

However, the Washington Monument turned out to be much more beautiful in its necessary simplicity than if it had a distracting building at the bottom.

Matisse painting hangs upside down

In 1961, Henri Matisse's painting *Le Bateau* hung upside down in New York's Museum of Modern Art.

It remained upside down for forty-one days until someone noticed.

It's estimated about 116,000 people passed in front of the painting before the error was noted.

Hans Christian Andersen had no children

One of the great writers of children's stories, Hans Christian Andersen was born in the slums of Odense, Denmark, in 1805.

He didn't receive any formal education until he was almost twenty years old, when he first entered grammar school.

Andersen eventually attended Copenhagen University and began writing children's poems, plays, and novels.

Among his most famous stories are "The Ugly Duckling," "The Emperor's New Clothes," and "The Little Mermaid."

Andersen died in 1875 without ever marrying, and this great children's writer never had any children of his own.

Some book notes

Fourteen years *before* the *Titanic* sank, Morgan Robertson wrote a fiction book about a ship named the "Titan" which has incredible similarities to the real *Titanic*. Both ships were on their maiden voyages; both were going from England to the U.S.; both hit an iceberg; and both sank in the approximate same spot in the North Atlantic.

The *World Almanac* got its name—not because it prints world facts—but because it was originally published by the *New York World* newspaper, and they used the name *World Almanac* to promote the newspaper.

In all the Perry Mason novels, Mason lost a case in only one: *The Case of the Terrified Typist*.

The most prolific painter

Pablo Picasso's career lasted seventy-eight years, from 1895 until his death in 1973.

He made more than 13,000 paintings and over 100,000 prints, engravings, and designs.

He also did over 300 sculptures and ceramics.

The value of Picasso's work has been valued at over $800 million.

Picasso used his mother's maiden name. His father's last name was Ruiz.

Horatio Alger no success

It's surprising to learn the true story of Horatio Alger.

Alger was the man who became famous for writing stories about poor boys who became rich. The very name "Horatio Alger" came to symbolize success.

But curiously, Horatio Alger himself had many personal problems, and he died broke. His writings inspired people to a better life—but Alger himself did not profit by it.

How the "Wizard of Oz" got his name

Frank Baum, who wrote *The Wizard of Oz*, chose the name of the wizard this way:

While writing the book, Baum was gazing around his office, trying to decide what to call the wizard. Baum saw the letters on his three file drawers across the room. One file read "A-G," the next "H-N," and the third "O-Z."

And "Oz" it became.

Five floors bigger than 102 floors

Although the Pentagon is only five stories high, it has more floor space than the Empire State Building in New York, which has 102 floors.

That was made possible by the Pentagon's unusual design of five rings on each of its five sides.

Despite being only five stories high, the Pentagon is one of the biggest office buildings in the world. It has over 3 million square feet of office space, and can house about 30,000 employees.

Father-son team does famous sculpture

The first sculptor to work on the sixty-foot-high faces of four U.S. Presidents on Mount Rushmore, South Dakota, was Gutzon Borglum.

He spent fourteen years, from 1927 to 1941, carving the faces of George Washington, Thomas Jefferson, Abraham Lincoln, and Theodore Roosevelt.

However, Gutzon Borglum died before the job was

completed. His son finished the work—and his son's first name was, appropriately, Lincoln.

The shortest correspondence ever written

French author Victor Hugo wrote his novel *Les Miserables* in 1862, and submitted it to his publisher.

Hugo was anxious to know how it was selling. He hadn't heard, and so he sent the following letter to his publisher, reprinted here in its entirety:

?

The publisher's answer was in keeping with Hugo's letter. The publisher wrote back, simply:

!

That was all that was needed to convey the message.

Dr. Doyle and Sherlock Holmes

Sherlock Holmes stories were created because the man who wrote them had failed as a doctor.

Sherlock Holmes books were written by Arthur Conan Doyle, who started his career as a physician. But so few patients came to see Doyle, he began writing stories in his office to pass the time. When the stories became popular, Doyle gave up medicine.

Doyle picked the name "Holmes" from American Oliver Wendell Holmes, whom Doyle admired.

Which country produces the Encyclopedia Britannica?

Despite its name, the Encyclopedia Britannica does not come from Britain now.

It originated in Great Britain in the eighteenth century. But a group of booksellers in the United States acquired its rights many years ago.

The Encyclopedia Britannica is now edited many miles from Britain—in Chicago, Illinois—and it's printed in the United States.

Eleven

Food

No ham in hamburgers

Since there's no ham in hamburgers, why are they called hamburgers?

To answer that question, you have to go back to the late 1800s, when a group of people came to the U.S. from Hamburg, Germany.

They brought with them a new custom—serving ground meat.

That kind of meat was soon named after their town— Hamburg. And that's how hamburgers got their name.

You've probably used Sylvan Goldman's invention—but don't know who he was

In 1937, a man named Sylvan Goldman owned a supermarket in Oklahoma City. He realized his customers weren't buying all the items they might, because they couldn't carry them all.

Goldman found the solution to the problem—he invented the supermarket shopping cart.

Food facts

Caesar salads are not named after Julius Caesar. They're named after a restaurant owner in Tijuana, Mexico—Caesar Gardini—who served the first one, in 1928.

Fig Newtons got their name because they were first made near the town of Newton, Massachusetts.

Cantaloupe is named after the town of Cantalupo, Italy, where it was first grown.

Alas, apple pie isn't originally American. It was first made in Europe.

On the other hand, Russian dressing isn't from Russia. It was first made in America.

M&M's candies took their name from their founders, Forrest Mars and Bruce Murrie.

Grapefruit has nothing to do with grapes

Why is grapefruit called grapefruit when it is not a grape?

Actually, grapefruit is not related in any way to grapes.

It got its name because it grows in bunches like grapes grow.

The story of potato chips

Potato chips were invented by chance.

In 1853, at the resort of Saratoga Springs, New York, a guest complained to a chef that his French fried potatoes were too thin. The chef, in anger, then cut potatoes as thin as possible to spite the guest—and found that people enjoyed them.

Thus, the potato chip was born. For many years, potato chips were called Saratoga chips after the place where they were invented.

A different George Washington invents instant coffee

One of the inventors of instant coffee was a man named George Washington—but it wasn't that George Washington.

This man was George C.L. Washington, born in Belgium in 1871. He came to the U.S. in 1896 and manufactured kerosene lamps. But the growing popularity of electricity hurt his business, and Washington went to Guatemala, where he worked on the idea for instant coffee.

You may have heard of his product, known as "G. Washington Coffee," which helped introduce instant coffee in the 1930s.

McDonald's named for two brothers

Richard and Maurice McDonald moved to California from New Hampshire and opened a movie house in Glendora.

But their theater drew smaller crowds than the nearby hot dog stand. They took the hint and started a hamburger stand in San Bernardino, in 1948.

One day a salesman, Ray Kroc of Chicago, stopped

and was impressed with the McDonald brothers' product and service.

Kroc suggested they open other restaurants together. But the McDonald brothers weren't interested.

Kroc bought out Richard and Maurice McDonald, and the rest, as they say, is history—and a lot of hamburgers.

Why are ice cream sundaes called sundaes?

In the nineteenth century, some communities made laws against certain pleasures on Sundays, and among those things outlawed were ice cream sodas.

To get around the law, a store in Evanston, Illinois, put ice cream in a dish, added flavoring—but no soda water—and called it an ice cream sundae.

To avoid offending some people, they changed the spelling from ice cream "sunday" to ice cream "sundae."

More food facts

Corned beef has nothing to do with corn. The word "corned" was an old word meaning "seasoned."

Popcorn was invented by the American Indians.

Chicken à la king was named after a real king, King Edward VII of England.

Bibb lettuce got its name from Major John Bibb of Kentucky, who developed that type of lettuce in the 1850s.

Fortune cookies, served for years at Chinese restaurants in America, were unknown in China until recent years.

Toll house cookies got their name from the Toll House

Inn in Massachusetts, where they were first made in 1930.

Why are sandwiches called sandwiches?

One of the world's most popular kinds of food was named after a man because he liked to play cards.

Sandwiches were named for England's Fourth Earl of Sandwich, John Montagu, who hated to stop playing cards to eat. So, he'd have his servant put meat between two slices of bread so he could eat and keep playing.

The Earl of Sandwich popularized this way of eating, and it's his name that's used millions of times every day when people order a sandwich.

When hot dogs were born

Harry Stevens was the concessionaire at the New York Giants' home baseball park, the Polo Grounds, in the late 1800s. One day it was cool and Stevens wasn't selling much of the cold food that was all they had at ballparks in those days.

During the game, he went shopping for something warm he could sell. He found a butcher shop and bought some warm sausages to serve the fans—but how could they hold them?

Stevens came up with the idea of holding the sausages in a bun—and the hot dog was born.

A New York newspaper cartoonist, Tad Dorgan, drew a picture of them, using a dachshund in the bun, and Dorgan named them "hot dogs."

The beginning of Cracker Jack

Cracker Jack was created by F. W. Rueckheim at the Chicago World's Fair in 1893. The recipe has never changed.

Cracker Jack got its name from a popular expression of the day. People used to say "crackerjack" to mean "great."

Sailor Jack on the box was modeled after Rueckheim's grandson and his dog Bingo.

The toy prize was added to Cracker Jack boxes in 1912.

Ice cream cones born by accident

At the World's Fair in St. Louis in 1904, a man selling ice cream ran out of dishes. In the next booth was a man selling waffles. The ice cream man borrowed some waffles and put the ice cream in the waffles.

He found that people enjoyed eating their ice cream held by a waffle—and the ice cream cone was born.

The first hamburgers-on-a-bun

In the year 1900, Louie Lassen owned a small restaurant in New Haven, Connecticut, called "Louie's Lunch."

Lassen was looking for a convenient way to serve nearby workers who wanted to take out and carry their hamburgers.

Lassen created the hamburger-on-a-bun.

How these foods got their names

Graham crackers were named after the Reverend Sylvester Graham, who advocated special diets in the 1800s.

Sanka coffee took its name from the French phrase *sans caffeine*, or without caffeine. They took the "san" from *sans* and the "ka" from the sound of the first two letters of caffeine.

Two vegetables are named after capital cities—lima beans for Lima, Peru, and brussels sprouts for Brussels, Belgium.

Eggs Benedict were named after a New York businessman, Sam Benedict, who dreamed up the combination one night at the Waldorf-Astoria Hotel.

Mayonnaise got its name from the Mediterranean city of Mahon, where it was first made.

The birth of pizza

Naples, Italy, was the birthplace of pizza.

Pizza was first made by a baker for the royal court in Naples in the 1700s.

Pizza's wide popularity in the United States didn't begin until after World War II, when returning GIs brought home the demand for pizza.

Twelve

Science, Weather, Inventions

A day is longer than a year

On the planet Venus, a day is longer than a year.

It takes Venus 247 of our days to turn around one time itself—but it takes Venus only 224 of our days to make its trip around the sun.

That makes every day longer than a year on Venus.

Hurricanes are typhoons and vice versa

There's no difference between a hurricane and a typhoon—with one exception.

They're both the same thing, except, by local custom, they're called hurricanes if they originate in the Atlantic or eastern Pacific oceans; and they're called typhoons if they originate in the western Pacific.

Bell wasn't trying to invent telephone

Alexander Graham Bell did not set out to invent the telephone.

Bell's wife and mother were hearing impaired, and

Bell was working on machines to help hard-of-hearing people hear better. Those experiments coincidentally led to the telephone.

Two other surprising facts about Bell: He was only twenty-nine when he invented the telephone. And Bell was so annoyed by the telephone in his later years that he had his own phone removed from his home!

Did Bell really invent telephone?

Although we've always heard that Alexander Graham Bell invented the telephone, at least two other inventors contested that opinion.

Elisha Gray filed a patent for a telephone the same day as Bell, but lost out in a legal fight.

Daniel Drawbaugh claimed he invented a telephone several years before Bell. Drawbaugh came close to convincing the Supreme Court, losing to Bell by a 4–3 decision.

Thus, instead of the Bell Telephone Company, we might have had the Gray or Drawbaugh Telephone Company.

Wintertime sun is closer

Oddly, in winter in the Northern Hemisphere, the Earth is closer to the sun than it is in summer.

Winter and summer are caused—not by the Earth moving closer or farther away from the sun—but by the tilt of the Earth.

Due to the earth's tilt, the Northern Hemisphere gets less sunlight than the Southern Hemisphere for half of each year; when this happens, it is winter in the north and summer in the south.

But for the other half of the year, the tilt of the earth brings the Northern Hemisphere more sunlight than the Southern Hemisphere. When this happens, it is summer in the north and winter in the south.

The tilt of the Earth is not directly related to the elliptical orbit of the Earth. This orbit happens to bring the Earth closer to the sun when the Northern Hemisphere is experiencing winter, and farther from the sun when the Northern Hemisphere is experiencing summer.

Unusual start for plastics industry

The entire plastics industry began because somebody was looking for a cheaper way to make billiard balls.

In the nineteenth century, billiard balls were made of natural ivory, and were very expensive. A manufacturer offered $10,000 to anyone who could make a substitute material that would still be tough enough.

A New York printer, John Hyatt, came up with the new material—plastics—for billiard balls, and that was the beginning of the plastics industry.

Ocean water isn't blue or green

If you ask the average person what the color of the ocean is, they'll probably answer blue or green—but that's not true.

Ocean water is not blue or green. It's colorless, like any other water. It's the same color as water from your spigot at home.

Oceans look blue or green only because of reflections from the sky above and vegetation below.

Horsepower is more power than a horse can exert

The word horsepower was originated by James Watt in 1783 to describe the working capability of his steam engine.

But Watt purposely inflated a real horse's power in comparison to his steam engine to be on the conservative side.

Each unit of power his steam engine could exert was one and a half times more than that of the strong draft horses that Watt used in his experiments.

Today, the standard unit of horsepower, used in such things as automobiles, is fifty percent more per unit than a real horse's power.

Some space facts

The crew of Apollo 11, which put the first men on the moon—Armstrong, Aldrin, and Collins—have the same initials as the biblical first men on earth—Adam, Abel, and Cain. Oddly, Buzz Aldrin's mother's maiden name was Moon.

The first words spoken from the surface of the moon were not the famous "one giant leap for mankind" speech, but "Houston, Tranquility Base here. The Eagle has landed."

On the planet Pluto, it is always night. The sun is so

far away, it appears as just a speck in the sky and does not bring daylight to Pluto.

The man who invented the Ferris wheel

A man with four names—George Washington Gale Ferris—gave his last name to Ferris wheels.

Ferris was an American engineer, specializing in bridge construction.

In 1893 he built the first Ferris wheel, which was used for the Columbian Exposition in Chicago. This Ferris wheel was 250 feet high and could carry 260 people.

Ferris died just three years later, at age thirty-seven.

How far can you see?

If you asked the average person how far they can see with the naked eye, you probably will get an answer that might range from a mile to several miles, depending on where they are.

Most people don't think about looking at the sky.

You can see 93 million miles when you look at the sun—because that's how far away it is.

And that's far from the limit of the average naked eye. At night you can see stars that are trillions of miles away.

Coldest day ever was in July

The coldest outdoor temperature ever recorded on earth was set in the month of July!

That coldest temperature was on July 22, 1983.

The reason it happened in July is because that's a winter month in the Southern Hemisphere, and the record low was set in Antarctica, which is in the Southern Hemisphere.

The all-time record low was reached when the thermometer plunged to 128 below zero Fahrenheit at Vostok, Antarctica.

Air-conditioning not invented to cool homes

When air-conditioning was invented in the early 1900s, it was *not* intended to cool homes or offices, or stores or theaters.

It was invented to control humidity in a printing plant, so printing paper would not expand or contract.

Only later did people realize that it would be effective in homes and other inside places. That was an afterthought.

Air-conditioning generally didn't come to homes until after World War II.

World's windiest spot is in New Hampshire

To realize how strong the wind has blown on New Hampshire's Mount Washington, consider this:

Winds over 74 mph are strong enough to be called hurricane force, but winds on Mount Washington, in April 1934, were recorded at 231 mph—and that's a world's record.

The mathematical odds on coin flips

If you flip a coin and heads come up ten straight times, many people would think on the eleventh flip, the odds would favor tails—but that isn't so.

As mathematicians point out, coins have no memory; therefore, the odds on the eleventh flip are 50–50 for heads or tails, just as on any flip, assuming the coin is okay.

Any time you flip a coin, the odds are even on heads or tails—regardless of what happened before.

The amazing coincidences of aluminum inventors

In 1886, Charles Hall of Thompson, Ohio, discovered the process that made production of aluminum practical, and he formed the Aluminum Company of America.

Meantime, Paul Heroult, working in Paris, discovered the same process in the same year as Hall did, even though they worked independently of each other. Heroult set up a European aluminum company.

What makes the coincidence even greater is that both Hall and Heroult were born in 1863; both discovered the aluminum process in 1886; both set up their own companies to manufacture aluminum in 1888; and both died in 1914.

Halley didn't discover Halley's Comet

The most famous comet is Halley's Comet—but it wasn't named after the man who discovered it.

Many scientists had observed the comet. However, it was named for Edmund Halley because he correctly predicted how often it would fly past Earth.

In 1705, he predicted the comet would return in 1758. It did, and was named in Halley's honor.

Halley said the comet would return every 76 years. It was here in 1986—and comes back in 2062.

How hot . . . and cold can it get in the U.S.?

The record for the highest outdoor temperature ever recorded in the U.S. was set on July 10, 1913 at Death Valley, California, when the thermometer hit 134 degrees Fahrenheit.

The record for the lowest temperature in the U.S. was set January 23, 1971, at Prospect Creek, Alaska. The thermometer plunged to 80 degrees below zero. The coldest day in a state other than Alaska was 70 below at Rogers Pass, Montana, on January 20, 1954.

The Earth spins—but we don't feel it

The Earth spins on its axis and moves around the sun—so why don't we feel anything?

The reason is that maintaining a constant speed has exactly the same effect as not moving at all; both are states of inertia. We can only feel *changes* in speed. So if the

Earth ever started to spin faster, or if it slowed down, we would certainly feel it.

The year without a summer

It happened in 1816.

The most powerful volcano in recorded history—Mount Tambora in the Dutch East Indies—sent so much debris into the atmosphere, it blocked the sun all around the Earth.

In many parts of the United States, temperatures dropped that summer. Snow fell in June. There was sleet and frost in July and August.

The year 1816 had no summer.

The inventor of the safety pin

One of history's most unusual inventors was Walter Hunt. He invented the safety pin and could have made millions of dollars, but sold the rights for just $400.

Hunt also threw away a fortune when he invented a sewing machine but didn't patent it.

Hunt still became rich by inventing a fire alarm, knife sharpener, ice breaker, and fountain pen. Not many people ever heard of Walter Hunt, but he was one of the most ingenious inventors.

U.S. gets more snow than the South Pole

Although the South Pole is the coldest spot on Earth, and is always packed with snow, it gets less snow each year than the United States.

Because of atmospheric conditions, it hardly ever snows at the South Pole.

However, the little snow they get doesn't melt. It stays there. But the South Pole, surprisingly, gets very little new snow each year.

The first flying saucers

The term "flying saucers" was born in 1947 when an airplane pilot saw unidentified flying objects over Mount Rainier in Washington State.

The pilot reported they looked like saucers.

Newspapers of the day jumped on that word "saucers"—and for the first time headlines across the country told of "flying saucers."

An underrated invention

Not many people think of the telegraph as one of history's most exciting inventions—but it gave humans something significant they never had before.

It's hard to realize now, but until the telegraph was invented in 1844, humans had *no* way to communicate instantly over any great distance. The telephone, radio, and TV were still years away.

The telegraph was the first instant long-distance communication system, and was really one of the landmark inventions in history.

That old tale about crickets is true

Amazingly, crickets really can tell you the temperature almost as accurately as a thermometer.

If you count the chirps a cricket makes in fifteen seconds, and then add the number 40, you will have the approximate temperature in degrees Fahrenheit.

Marie Curie's unique scientific achievements

Marie Curie is the only person in history to win the Nobel Prize in both physics and chemistry—and she and her husband and daughter collected four Nobel Prizes in all.

She was born Marie Sklodowska in Poland in 1867, and became a brilliant student in mathematics, physics, and chemistry, eventually enrolling in the Sorbonne in Paris.

In 1895 she married a French scientist, Pierre Curie, and they began the studies that led to each winning the Nobel Prize in physics in 1903 for their work with radioactivity.

Marie Curie won another Nobel Prize, for chemistry, in 1911 after her husband's death. That Nobel was based on her studies of the chemistry of radium.

Her daughter, Irene, was awarded the Nobel Prize for chemistry in 1935 for her work on the synthesis of new radioactive elements.

Astronaut hurt in bathtub

Ironically, the first American astronaut to orbit the Earth, John Glenn, survived his launch from Cape Canaveral, his space flight, and his reentry to Earth, but then later suffered a serious injury.

His serious injury occurred—not on any dangerous space mission—but when he slipped and fell in his bathtub at home. It put him out of work for some time.

John Glenn survived the unknown of space, and then got hurt in the familiar comfort of his house.

That popular snowflake theory

For years, most of us have been told that no two snowflakes are alike, and most people probably believe that.

But there can't be any proof of that until every snowflake that falls everywhere in the world is examined. And that, of course, can't be done.

Some will say mathematical probability dictates that since no two snowflakes have yet been found that are alike, it indicates the theory is correct.

But we really don't know because they all haven't been checked. Maybe somewhere there's been a snowflake just like another snowflake.

The man who invented sign language

Although Louis Braille is well known for inventing the Braille system for the blind, the person who invented sign language for the deaf is hardly remembered today.

The person who created the single-hand alphabet and sign language for the deaf was Abbé de L'Epee.

De L'Epee developed sign language at a school for the deaf in Paris in the eighteenth century. Unfortunately, his name is not attached to it as Braille's name is for the Braille system for the blind.

Biggest snowfall

The greatest one-day snowfall in the United States in the history of Weather Bureau records was at Silver Lake, Colorado, on April 14, 1921.

It snowed 76 inches in twenty-four hours.

Days whiz by on Jupiter

The planet Jupiter spins so fast, there is a new sunrise about every ten hours.

Jupiter has more than twice as many days and nights as Earth in the same amount of time.

Jupiter spins much faster than any other planet. There are more sunrises and more sunsets on Jupiter than on any other planet in the Solar system.

King invents safety razor

The person who invented the safety razor for shaving was an American named King Gillette.

King was his real first name. His full name was King Camp Gillette.

He was born in 1855 and invented the safety razor in

the early 1900s, forming the Gillette Safety Razor Company.

King Gillette was also an author and wrote *Human Drift* and *The People's Corporation*.

The mysterious death of Diesel

Rudolf Diesel developed the engine that bears his name today.

He was a German inventor, born in 1858. He studied mechanical engineering and later worked under several prominent physicists in Germany and Switzerland.

Diesel patented the diesel engine in 1892, and founded a factory to make the engines.

He mysteriously disappeared from a Channel steamer while crossing from England to Belgium in 1913, and his body was never found, nor was it known under what circumstances he died.

The coincidence of the sun and moon

An amazing coincidence makes the sun and the moon appear to be about the same size—even though the sun is much larger than the moon.

It just so happens that while the sun is about 400 times bigger than the moon, it is also—coincidentally—about 400 times farther away from us than the moon.

Because of that, they appear to be the same size.

The man who invented champagne

Champagne was invented by a Benedictine monk.

He was Dom Pérignon. He was put in charge of the vineyards at his monastery in 1668, and developed sparkling wines.

Champagne got its name because the monastery was in the Champagne section of France.

The mystery of the night sky

A question—still unsolved—is why the night sky is dark—and not light. Here's why that's a mystery:

Some scientists feel that with the billions of stars in the sky, those stars should produce enough light to make our night sky bright. But despite all those bright stars, our night skies are dark.

No satisfactory, generally-accepted theory has yet been made as to why there's not more light in our night sky.

The lightning myth

It's often said that lightning never strikes the same place twice, but that's absolutely not true.

In fact, lightning *likes* to strike the same place twice. Lightning will actually seek out those places or things that attract lightning.

For example, the radio mast on top of the Empire State Building in New York has been hit by lightning more than fifty times.

Lightning can—and does—strike the same place twice, or more.

Volts and voltage named for a count

Alessandro Volta was an Italian physicist born in Como, Italy, in 1745.

He experimented in electricity beginning in the 1760s and discovered constant-current electricity in 1800, opening a new electrical age. He also invented the electric battery and electric condenser.

For his work he was given the title of Count and went by the name of Count Volta until his death in 1827.

The volt and voltage, units of electrical measurements, were named after him in 1881.

Equal opportunity hurricanes

The custom of naming hurricanes after women began in World War II.

Before that, hurricanes had no names. But homesick sailors during the war started naming hurricanes after girlfriends back home.

That custom continued until 1978, when some thought it unfair to name devastating hurricanes only after women. In 1978, the U.S. Weather Service began using men's names as well as women's for hurricanes.

The unusual background of Samuel F.B. Morse

Samuel F.B. Morse, who invented the telegraph, and for whom the Morse code was named, spent much of his early career in a field far removed from science and inventions.

Before Morse graduated from Yale in 1810, he was painting portraits, and after graduation, he made a painting of Marquis de Lafayette that hung for many years in the New York City Hall.

Morse went to England to study art. He returned to become a professor of painting and sculpture at New York University in 1832.

But while at NYU, he began to experiment with possibilities of the telegraph after becoming interested in uses of electricity.

Eight years later he received the patent for the telegraph.

Thirteen

Animals

The biggest animals that ever lived

Contrary to popular belief, the biggest animals in the history of the Earth were not dinosaurs.

The biggest animals that ever lived are today's blue whales.

Some blue whales are more than 100 feet long and weigh 150 tons.

The biggest dinosaurs were only about ninety feet in length and 50 tons in weight.

If ever an animal had the right name ... this is it

No animal in the world can travel as fast under its own power as the bird known as the swift.

Swifts can fly at speeds of 100 mph.

Not only that, but they can fly many hours without stopping. Some swifts spend most of their lives airborne. They eat by catching insects in the air, and they mate while flying.

Swifts rarely alight on the ground. When they do stop

flying, they usually perch on a tree or some other high object.

Nature has given swifts an ideal body for flying. The special structure of their wings coupled with powerful breast muscles make possible their rapid, sustained flight.

Those weren't buffaloes

Contrary to popular opinion, large herds of buffalo never roamed North America in the early days of the nation.

The animals mistakenly called buffaloes in America were technically bisons. The true buffalo—a native of only Africa and Asia—has long horns. The American bison, which many people called a buffalo, has shorter horns and a more pointed back.

Maybe Buffalo Bill should have been called "Bison Bill."

Which came first—chicken or egg?

According to *National Geographic*, scientists have settled the old dispute over which came first—the chicken or the egg.

They say that reptiles were laying eggs thousands of years before chickens appeared, and the first chicken came from an egg laid by a bird that was not quite a chicken. That seems to answer the question. The egg came first.

Babies are bigger than their parents

Baby eagles quickly grow to become bigger than their parents. But then, as eagles mature, they lose plumage and weight. This lets them fly better when they go out on their own to become parents themselves.

So, as eagles approach parenthood, their size is reduced, and the cycle starts over with baby eagles being bigger than their parents.

This animal has different name twice a year

There's one kind of animal that's known by one name in winter and an entirely different name in summer.

In winter, ermines have a white coat and they're called ermines.

But in summer their coats change to brown and they are known then as weasels.

Turkeys have nothing to do with Turkey

Turkeys do not come from the country of Turkey.

Turkeys are native American birds, and, in fact, there were never any turkeys in Turkey until they were brought there from America.

Turkeys were named by English settlers in America. They thought the birds looked like guinea hens from Turkey. But the turkey is a separate, all-American species.

Benjamin Franklin wanted the turkey—instead of the eagle—to be the American symbol.

Humans could not live without insects & other invertebrates

Although many humans don't like insects, spiders, worms, bugs, and other creepy crawlers, some ecologists say the human race would perish quickly without them.

Those insects and other invertebrates maintain the soil structure and fertility on which plant growth and thus all higher organisms depend.

They cycle nutrients, pollinate crops and other plants, disperse seeds, keep harmful organisms under control, and eliminate wastes.

Ecologists have gone so far as to say that if all invertebrates disappeared, humans would last on Earth for only a few months.

The big bird mystery

One of the great mysteries of the animal world is how so many birds can fly hundreds, or thousands, of miles to exact locations without losing their way.

Long-flying birds often can't see the ground because of either the weather or the fact that they fly at night. Weather also prevents them at times from seeing stars, or other possible guideposts.

How do they do it? Scientists are still trying to find out.

Which animals have best memory?

You often hear the expression that someone has a memory like an elephant, or that an elephant never forgets, but among all animals, elephants do not have the best memory.

According to recent research, other animals have better memories than elephants.

Besides humans, dolphins and monkeys have the best memory.

Some animal facts

Moths do not eat clothes; it's the caterpillar from moth eggs that eats clothes. But full-grown moths do not.

Although greyhound dogs are used in dog racing, they are not the fastest-running dogs. Salukis can run faster than greyhounds.

One of the oddities of nature is that while whales and porpoises live under water, they need air. They must spend their lives continuously coming to the surface for air before returning underwater.

Although beavers live near rivers, streams, and lakes, they never eat fish.

Ants are found on every continent in the world except the one continent that start with the letters "ant"— Antarctica.

Great weather for ducks?

Although many people say rainy weather is "great weather for ducks," scientists say that's not true.

They say that, first of all, ducks don't like to be in the rain any more than people do. Heavy rain can actually be dangerous to young ducks, causing damage to their feathers.

The next time it rains, it's probably a good idea not to say it's great weather for ducks.

The biggest eyes in the world

One of the most unusual animals found anywhere is the giant squid.

Giant squids don't have just eight arms like the octopus. Squids have ten arms.

But the most amazing thing about giant squids is their size. They're as big as 55 feet long—and they have eyes bigger than basketballs, measuring some fifteen inches across, the biggest eyes of any animal in the world.

Males carry the baby

Fish known as sea horses are unique. They are carried and given birth by the male.

Female sea horses lay eggs—but then the males carry the eggs in a pouch on their bodies until the eggs hatch.

Sea horses are also the only fish that swim upright.

Another fact about sea horses is that their heads,

which resemble tiny horses, are sometimes preserved, fitted on wooden bases, and used as knights in chess.

Lobsters not red

Although many people associate lobsters with the color red—and color pictures or drawings of lobsters are usually red—that is not their native color.

Lobsters are greenish or bluish. They become red only when they are boiled.

This animal can't go forward

There's one kind of animal in the world that can walk only backward.

It's the ant lion, or as it's sometimes called, the doodlebug.

Ant lions are small insects that usually live on dry, sandy soil. They dig holes in the soil to trap other insects for food—and they dig those holes by walking around backward.

Ant lions cannot walk forward, and they are the only known animals that spend their lives walking backward.

Some animal myths

The sayings "busy as a beaver" and "blind as a bat" have developed from false information—because beavers don't work that much, and bats can "see" better than most other animals.

Beavers work only when necessary, and easily lose their desire to work hard.

And bats, through their own radar-type system, can fly in utter darkness, yet avoid obstacles and spot even the smallest of insects.

Bulls will charge green too

Contrary to popular opinion, bulls don't get mad when they see red—bulls are color blind.

Tests have proven that bulls will charge yellow or blue or green or any other color just as much as they will charge red.

The reason red capes are used in bullfighting is just tradition, but in reality the color red has no effect on the bull's performance.

Not much of a life for mayfly

One of the strangest of all animals is the insect known as the mayfly.

Most mayflies live less than a day and never eat in their adulthood.

The lifetime of mayflies usually begins in late afternoon when they emerge from their eggs. They fly for the first time, mate, lay eggs themselves, and die before dawn—having spent less than twenty-four hours on Earth.

Surprising facts about the ostrich

The saying that ostriches hide their heads in sand is a myth. When in danger, ostriches are tough fighters. Instead of hiding their heads, they will stand and fight or use their great speed to flee an opponent.

Ostriches are such fast runners, they can outrun a horse.

Male ostriches can roar like lions.

Ostriches are the biggest birds in the world, and they have a longer life span than other birds. Ostriches live as long as seventy years.

The amazing penguins

One of the oddities of nature is that penguins, who are able to thrive in the bitter cold of the South Pole, can also live just as easily in the heat of the equator.

Besides the South Pole, penguins are also natives of the Galapagos Islands, which are on the equator.

It's amazing that penguins can survive in both Antarctica and at the equator, but they do.

The strange life of the cicada

One of the most unusual forms of life in the world are cicadas, or as they're sometimes called, seventeen-year locusts.

As soon as these cicadas are born, they burrow into the ground—and they stay in the ground, developing, for seventeen years.

At the end of this time they emerge from the ground, fully grown, and are ready to live as adults. But they live aboveground only a few weeks, just enough time to reproduce and die.

Who said mice love cheese?

Contrary to popular opinion, mice do not love cheese.

A hungry mouse will eat cheese—just as they will eat almost anything—but recent laboratory tests show that when given a choice, mice will choose foods other than cheese.

Mice seem to like candy, for instance, better than cheese, and a professional exterminator recommends candy instead of cheese for mousetraps.

Dog days have nothing to do with dogs

Days in August known as "dog days" got their name not from dogs on Earth, but from a star in the sky.

The star Sirius is called the "Dog Star" because the ancient Greeks, who named many of the stars, thought Sirius helped form the outline of a dog in its constellation.

Sirius, the Dog Star, used to appear prominently in August, so those days were called "dog days."

More animal facts

When armadillos give birth, it is almost always to identical quadruplets.

Fish can never close their eyes. They have no eyelids.

Even though elephants have larger ears than any other animal, they have poor hearing.

Some flat fish, such as the flounder, have their two eyes on the same side of their head. They're born with an eye on each side, but as they mature, one eye moves until it rests close to the other eye.

Do birds "eat like a bird"?

When a human eats a small amount of food, you sometimes hear the expression "He or she eats like a bird," implying that birds don't eat much.

What a misconception that is.

Many birds eat as much as twice their weight a day. That would be the same as a 150-pound human eating 300 pounds of food daily.

Birds don't "eat like a bird."

Fourteen

TV, Radio, Newspapers

CBS and ABC had different names

Both the CBS and ABC networks had different names when they started.

CBS was formed in 1927. It was originally named UIB, or United Independent Broadcasters.

And until 1943, ABC was part of NBC.

Originally, NBC owned two networks—the NBC Blue and the NBC Red networks. The government made NBC give up one of them. NBC Blue became a separate company, and changed its name to ABC.

The name of crossword puzzles an accident

Arthur Wynn, the man who invented crossword puzzles, originally called them "wordcross" puzzles—but a printing error made it come out "crossword" instead of "wordcross."

Since it appeared that way in the newspaper the first day, it was decided to let it remain in that form.

Thus, one of our most famous expressions exists by accident.

Nobody thought of selling commercials on radio

The first commercial ever broadcast over radio was for the Queensboro Realty Company, on station WEAF in New York in 1922—and the oddity is that radio broadcasting was two years old before anybody thought of putting advertisements on the air.

When broadcasting started in 1920, most stations were owned by radio manufacturers. They expected to make money only by selling more radios. It took two years until somebody realized money could also be made by selling commercials on the air.

Why are TV awards called "Emmys"?

The Emmy Awards got their name from a nickname.

Emmy is a variation of the nickname used in the early days of TV for the image orthicon tube, which made TV possible.

The image orthicon tube was called an "immy," which began to be pronounced as "emmy."

TV, looking for something to match the movies' Oscars, chose the word "Emmy" for its awards. The name was suggested by Harry Lubcke, who was president of the National Academy of TV Arts.

The first Emmy Awards were given in 1949.

The three estates before the press

If the press is called the Fourth Estate, what are the first three estates?

In the Middle Ages, the nobility was called the First Estate; the clergy, the Second; and property owners, the Third Estate.

When did TV start?

The first place in the world that had regular nightly programs on television was England. Their TV service was started by the British Broadcasting Corporation on November 2, 1936.

Regular TV shows did not come to the United States until 1939, when several experimental stations began in New York City and Schenectady, New York.

The first sports event ever televised was a Columbia-Princeton baseball game on May 17, 1939, from Baker Field in New York. Bill Stern was the announcer. W2XBS, a forerunner of WNBC, broadcast the event.

The sale of TV sets and the development of television programming was mostly curtailed by World War II, and it wasn't until after the war that TV became a mass medium.

As late as 1948, only two percent of American homes had TV sets.

The first coast-to-coast TV in the U.S. began on September 4, 1951, when President Harry Truman addressed the nation from San Francisco on the signing of the Japanese Peace Treaty.

Regular color TV started in 1953.

Top TV shows of the fifties, sixties, and seventies

Here are the top-rated national TV shows in the decades of the fifties, sixties, and seventies:

In the fifties, it was Milton Berle's *Texaco Star Theater*, *I Love Lucy*, *Arthur Godfrey*, *The $64,000 Question*, and *Gunsmoke*.

In the sixties it was *Gunsmoke*, *Wagon Train*, *The Beverly Hillbillies*, *Bonanza*, *Andy Griffith*, and *Laugh-In*.

In the seventies: *All in the Family*, *Marcus Welby M.D.*, *Happy Days*, *Laverne & Shirley*, and *Three's Company*.

George Washington and others gave no news conferences

The presidential news conferences, which have become a vital part of U.S. democracy, were unknown until the twentieth century. Early Presidents merely handed statements to the press, or limited themselves to talking with only selected or favored newspeople.

The first President to hold a general news conference was Woodrow Wilson, in 1913.

Even then the practice was not to quote a President directly. And questions often had to be submitted in advance, with the President answering only the ones he wanted to deal with.

The first presidential press conference at which direct quotations were allowed was on December 16, 1953, with President Eisenhower. The entire conference was printed in some newspapers, and it was also broadcast.

In the golden age of radio, there was no FM

When radio was the major broadcasting medium, before TV, in the 1920s and 1930s, all radio stations were on the AM, or amplitude modulation, band.

But Edwin Armstrong found another method of sending radio signals and started an experimental station in Alpine, New Jersey, in 1939, using FM, or frequency modulation.

The growth of FM was slow because existing radio sets could not receive it. People had to buy new, special radios to get FM.

It was not until the 1950s that manufacturers began mass marketing of FM radios, and more and more stations began broadcasting on the FM band.

Television's development helped by teenage inventor

One of the key principles that made the invention of television possible was developed by a high school student.

In 1922, Philo Farnsworth of Beaver, Utah, then sixteen years old, worked on experiments and found a way to send pictures through the air with his discovery of an image dissector. At the urging of his high school principal, Farnsworth sold his invention to RCA. This high school sophomore played an important part in the creation of TV.

As an adult, Farnsworth formed a research lab, the Farnsworth TV and Radio Company, which later became part of the International Telephone & Telegraph Company.

Oldest newspaper in the U.S.

The oldest continuously published newspaper in America is the *Hartford* (Connecticut) *Courant*.

It was established in 1764, originally as a weekly.

In 1836 it became a daily newspaper.

Why was it called *M*A*S*H?

One of the most popular television series in history was *M°A°S°H*. Its final episode in its original run, on February 28, 1983, drew the highest Nielsen rating up to that time, with sixty percent of all households with a TV set watching.

The name of the program came from the initials of the words Mobile Army Surgical Hospital.

Radio was invented for different purpose

When radio was invented, people said it would never last because its original idea was to let one person talk to, or communicate with, another person—as on a telephone—but it was felt that too many people could listen in.

There was no privacy on radio, as there was on a telephone.

Few saw the advantage of having many people listen.

Few saw the prospect of radio becoming a mass medium of news and entertainment.

Ironically, radio was invented for one use—but became successful because it was eventually used for a different purpose than its inventors intended.

Radio-TV-newspaper facts

The first scheduled radio broadcast in history was the presidential election returns on KDKA, Pittsburgh, on November 2, 1920.

The comic strip "Peanuts" originally had a different name. It was first called "Li'l Folks."

The three-tone musical chime used for many years by NBC as its trademark sound is composed of three notes—G, E, and C—which stand for one of NBC's original owners, the General Electric Co.

Television almost had a different name. Some early developers called it "radio-vision," and that almost became its permanent name.

What was the first commercial ever broadcast on TV?

The first commercial ever broadcast over television was on July 1, 1941 over WNBT in New York, the predecessor of WNBC.

The camera focused on a wristwatch, and the announcer said, "It's ten minutes after ten, Bulova watch time."

The commercial cost Bulova nine dollars.

How soap operas got their name

In the heyday of network radio in the 1930s and 1940s, fifteen-minute daily serial dramas filled the afternoon air.

Among the longtime favorites were "Ma Perkins," "Our Gal Sunday," "Backstage Wife," "Just Plain Bill," "Pepper Young's Family," and "Young Widder Brown."

They came to be called soap operas because most of them were sponsored by soap companies.

How cable TV started

In 1947, John Walson, Sr., of Mahanoy City, Pennsylvania, owned an appliance store.

He was having trouble selling television sets because the mountains of eastern Pennsylvania interfered with reception.

He built an antenna on the top of a nearby mountain and ran a cable to TV sets in his store window.

Walson then persuaded residents to hook up to his cable system in their homes for a $100 installation fee and two dollars a month.

Walson eventually owned a large cable TV company in Pennsylvania and New Jersey. He was recognized by the National Cable TV Association in 1979 as the pioneer of cable TV.

Fifteen

Health

Original senior citizens were teenagers

In the early years of the human race, people lived, on the average, to be only sixteen or seventeen years of age.

Life span has steadily increased. In the Stone Age, the average human lived to be about twenty-six. From the fifth to the ninth centuries, the average life span was thirty-six.

In 1900, the average American lived forty-seven years. Today, the average is over seventy.

Why are X rays called X rays?

X rays got their name when Dr. Wilhelm Roentgen, a professor of physics in Germany, discovered the X-ray process in 1895.

He wasn't sure then exactly what made the X-ray pictures possible—and since the letter X is often used in science for the unknown, he called them the "X rays."

Some medical facts

Plastic surgery has nothing to do with plastics. In fact, plastic surgery existed long before the invention of plastics. The word comes from the Greek "plastikos," which means to mold or to shape.

In the human body, the small intestine is about four times longer than the large intestine.

Contrary to popular opinion, newborn babies cannot shed tears. Babies don't cry with tears until approximately three months of age.

Alzheimer's disease was named after Dr. Alois Alzheimer, who did research on the disease in the early 1900s.

Hay fever has nothing to do with hay, and it's not a fever.

Our magnificent brain

The human brain weighs only about three pounds—yet it holds more than 10 billion cells.

Our little three-pound brain, incredibly, contains all of a person's memory, reasoning, consciousness, and emotions.

No computer can compare with the brain. The human brain is the most complex machine ever made.

Are cesarean births named for Julius Caesar?

It is a commonly held belief that cesarean sections got their name from Julius Caesar, but some historians point out that nobody really knows if Caesar was born that way.

In fact, no one is sure today if cesarean sections were even performed when he was born in about 100 B.C.

There are at least two other theories about where the name came from. One is that the name is derived from the Latin word *caedere*, or *caesura*, which means to cut.

Another theory is that under Roman law, called Lex Caesuras, dying women were required to be operated on in the last weeks of pregnancy in an effort to save the child.

A variety of authorities now dispute that cesarean sections were named for Julius Caesar.

They overcame handicaps

Horatio Nelson won great naval battles despite having lost his right arm and right eye.

Sarah Bernhardt continued being a great stage actress after she lost a leg.

Sir Walter Scott wrote some of his best books while in almost unbearable pain from a paralytic stroke.

Glenn Cunningham was the greatest mile runner in the world after having his legs burned badly in childhood. Cunningham began to run to strengthen his legs, and he became a champion.

Turtles take it easy and outlive humans

Human beings, with all their intelligence and medical knowledge, cannot outlive the turtle.

Some turtles are known to have lived past the age of 150. Many live more than a hundred years.

Turtles don't have the benefit of modern medical science to keep them long-lived. How do they have such long life spans?

They are one of the slowest-moving animals in the world. Maybe there's a lesson here.

Do more accidents occur at home or outside the home?

According to insurance statistics, more accidents occur each year in the home.

You'd think you'd be safer by simply staying home— but figures continually show that more people get injured in their homes than anywhere else.

There are about twice as many accidents every year in the home than there are in cars or planes or at work.

Human heart not heart-shaped

The human heart does not look quite like those heart-shaped drawings we always see.

The heart of a human being looks more than anything else like the shape of a person's fist.

Another misconception is the location of the heart.

You often hear the heart is on the left side of the chest. It's really just about in the middle of the chest.

Babies weren't born in hospitals

Jimmy Carter, the U.S. President from 1977 to 1981, was the first U.S. President to be born in a hospital.

Carter was born in 1924. All previous Presidents were born at home.

That was the custom until well into the twentieth century.

Sharks may help human health

Although sharks are often considered enemies of humans, sharks could hold a key to making humans healthier.

Sharks apparently are the only animals who never get sick. As far as is known, they are immune to every disease, including cancer.

Researchers are trying to determine what chemical or other component gives sharks their fabulous immunity. It's hoped such a discovery could possibly be adapted to the human body.

Incredible fact about human body

Here's one of those facts that sounds unbelievable—but it's true.

The human body has about 100,000 miles of blood vessels.

If all the blood vessels in your body were straightened

out and placed end to end, they would reach 100,000 miles—or around the world four times.

It seems inconceivable that a human body could hold that many blood vessels, but it does.

Do doctors love snakes?

The symbol of the medical profession—the caduceus—is a rod that has wings and snakes.

Why would doctors display snakes on their emblem?

It comes from mythology, where the caduceus was a magic wand used to control the lives of people.

The wand had snakes on it because, according to one theory, snakes shed their skins each year for new skin—representing renewal.

Another theory is that Mercury or Hermes in mythology threw the wand between two fighting snakes; they wound themselves around it and came face-to-face as friends.

The wand eventually came to be a symbol for Aesculapius, the Greco-Roman god of medicine.

What is it about cigar smokers?

While evidence seems to prove the dangers of cigarette smoking to health, there are a number of famous cigar smokers who lived abnormally long lives.

Winston Churchill died at age ninety-one.

Field Marshal Montgomery died at eighty-nine.

Arthur Rubenstein at ninety-five.

Groucho Marx at eighty-seven.

Sigmund Freud at eighty-three.

Somerset Maugham at ninety-one.

Bernard Baruch at ninety-five.

Tip O'Neill at eighty-one.

Zino Davidoff, who promoted, sold, and smoked cigars, died in 1994 at age eighty-seven.

And, at this writing, George Burns is still living at age ninety-eight.

More medical facts

Humans have about twelve pints of blood in their bodies.

"RX" on a prescription is the Latin abbreviation for "recipe."

Most cases of Rocky Mountain spotted fever do not occur in the Rocky Mountain area.

More people died of influenza in World War I than were killed in battle.

The funny bone is neither funny nor a bone. It's a nerve—but it is located near the humerus bone in the arm.

Sixteen

Colleges

Ivy League schools had different names

Seven of the eight Ivy League colleges originally had different names than they do today.

Brown was Rhode Island College; Columbia was King's College; Dartmouth was Wheelock's School; Harvard was Cambridge; Penn was Franklin's Academy; Princeton was the College of New Jersey; and Yale was the Collegiate School.

Of all Ivy League schools, only Cornell has had the same name throughout its history.

No college for nine Presidents

Nine U.S. Presidents never went to college—and in that group of nine are two men who are often rated among the greatest Presidents of all time, George Washington and Abraham Lincoln.

The other seven Presidents who never attended college were Andrew Jackson, Martin Van Buren, Zachary Taylor, Millard Fillmore, Andrew Johnson, Grover Cleveland, and Harry Truman.

College named for teenager

A major university in the U.S. is named after a fifteen-year-old boy.

It's Stanford University in Palo Alto, California.

Stanford was named for Leland Stanford, Jr., who died at the age of fifteen.

His father, railroad tycoon Leland Stanford, Sr., gave money to the school to honor his son's memory.

Stanford University, thus, is the only major university in the country named in honor of a teenage boy.

Some college facts

The first college to use the word "campus" to describe its grounds was Princeton. "Campus" is Latin for "field."

The largest Catholic university in America isn't Notre Dame, but Boston College.

Boston College's address isn't Boston, but rather Chestnut Hill, Massachusetts.

Likewise, the University of Miami is technically not in Miami, but in Coral Gables, Florida.

The term "Ivy League" wasn't coined by the colleges involved, but by the sports pages of the New York *Herald Tribune* in the 1930s.

John Harvard's small gift

Can you imagine a great university naming itself after someone just because he gave them 260 books and $2000?

That's about all John Harvard gave Harvard College—and they named the school after him.

When John Harvard died in 1638, he left his books and about $2000 to the college, then called Cambridge.

They needed the money and books so badly, they named the whole school in his honor.

Beer U.

If ever college kids had a right to drink beer, it would be the students at Vassar College in Poughkeepsie, N.Y.

Vassar was founded as Vassar Female College in 1861 and changed its name to Vassar College in 1867.

Vassar became one of the leading women's colleges in America. For many years it was an all-women's school, but it began admitting men in 1969.

The school was created by Matthew Vassar with a gift of $408,000, a great fortune when Vassar donated it in the 1860s.

Matthew Vassar had made his money ... as a beer maker. He owned a prosperous brewery in Poughkeepsie.

The Class of '24 at Bowdoin

One of the most remarkable graduating classes of all time was the Class of 1824 at little Bowdoin College in Brunswick, Maine.

In that small class was one man who became President of the United States, Franklin Pierce—and two men who became world-famous authors, Henry Wadsworth Longfellow and Nathaniel Hawthorne.

Why a "Bachelor's" degree?

Ever wonder why a college degree is called a "Bachelor's" degree?

The original meaning of a bachelor was a young apprentice. And since the college Bachelor's degree is the
first degree issued, coming before a Master's or Doctor's
degree, that first degree became known as a Bachelor's
degree.

Second-oldest U.S. college?

It's easy to guess that Harvard is the oldest college in the
U.S. Harvard was founded in 1636. But naming the
second-oldest U.S. college is more difficult.

It is William & Mary, founded in Williamsburg, Virginia, in 1693.

Despite its male-female name, William & Mary did
not admit women as students for its first 225 years, or
until 1918.

Nicholas Brown got a lot of publicity for $5000

The Ivy League college Brown University got its name in
an unusual way.

It was originally named Rhode Island College, in 1764.

But after the Revolutionary War, they advertised they
would rename the college after any person who could
help by donating $6000.

A businessman—Nicholas Brown—offered to give the school $5000.

The school needed the money, and apparently no one offered more, so they named the *whole* college after Brown and his $5000.

The irony of Oxford University's name

The prestigious Oxford University in England got its name from one of the least intelligent animals, the ox.

Oxford took its name from its location, which is situated in an area where oxen used to ford, or cross, a river. The place was known as "Oxford"—taken from "ox" and "ford."

Oxford University was founded in the fourteenth century, and it is where Rhodes scholars come to study.

The state universities

Originally almost all colleges in the U.S. were either private or church-supported.

But Congressman Justin Morrill of Vermont sponsored a bill in 1862 that gave land and money to the states for the purpose of establishing state universities to teach agriculture and mechanical arts.

Morrill's bill was called the Morrill, or Land Grant Act, and was the forerunner of today's vast network of state universities throughout the country.

An amazing college class

There's probably never been a college class like the Class of 1791 at Hampden-Sydney College in Hampden-Sydney, Virginia.

In that class, there were just eight students, but one became a U.S. Senator, one a U.S. congressman, one a state senator, one a state representative, one a college president, one a cabinet member, and one a judge.

The eighth student in that class dropped out in his senior year, but went on to become President of the United States—William Henry Harrison.

Northwestern University is not in the Northwest

Why in the world is Northwestern University, in Evanston, Illinois, called Northwestern? It's far from the Northwest.

The story begins in 1787, when Illinois was made part of what was then called the Northwest Territory.

That name came from the fact that Illinois was north of the Ohio River and west of Pennsylvania—a designation made by Congress in the days when the United States had not yet extended to the Pacific and to what is now called the Northwest.

The university opened in 1855 and chose its name because it said it would serve the people of the original Northwest Territory.

Little William & Mary produces second-most Presidents

Although William & Mary College in Williamsburg, Virginia, is not the largest or most famous college in America, it has produced the second-most U.S. Presidents among all U.S. colleges.

Not surprisingly, Harvard has produced the most U.S. Presidents. Five future Presidents went to Harvard—John Adams, John Quincy Adams, Theodore Roosevelt, Franklin Roosevelt, and John Kennedy.

But next comes William & Mary. Three future Presidents went to William & Mary—Thomas Jefferson, James Monroe, and John Tyler.

The biggest university

The university that has the greatest enrollment in the United States is the State University of New York.

It has over 400,000 students at sixty-four campuses throughout the state.

The university with the most students at one site is Ohio State in Columbus, which has an enrollment of over 50,000.

The largest school building in America is the Cathedral of Learning at the University of Pittsburgh. It is a 42-story skyscraper with over 1200 rooms.

Seventeen

Time, Days, Months, Years, Holidays

Months have wrong names

September, October, November, and December are mis-named.

According to their Latin derivation, September means seventh month; October means eighth; November means ninth; and December means tenth month—but September is our ninth month, October is tenth, November is eleventh, and December is the twelfth month.

The confusion came when the calendar was changed in the 1700s from the Roman to the present-day Gregorian calendar. When that happened, the positions of the months changed. September, for instance, moved from being the seventh month to being the ninth month.

Those months all moved—but their inaccurate names remain.

February was robbed

Why does February have only 28 days (or 29 in leap years), while all other months have either 30 or 31 days?

Originally, February had 30 days. But Julius Caesar took one day from February and added it to the month named after him—July. That changed July from 30 to 31 days.

Later, the Emperor Augustus took another day from February. He added it to the month named for him—August, giving that month 31 days, and leaving February with only 28, or 29 in leap years.

New Year's Day was in March

New Year's Day was once celebrated in America—not in January—but in March.

New Year's Day was on March 25.

It wasn't changed to January 1 until England and the American colonies scrapped the old calendar and adopted the present calendar in 1752.

Maybe March 25 is a more logical time for New Year's, after all.

March heralds the beginning of spring—and that's really more of a new year than January 1.

What's the longest month?

We know February is the shortest month of the year—but what's the longest month?

Many people guess June because it has the longest day of the year. But it's not the longest month. June has just 30 days.

For all states with daylight savings time, the answer is October. October has 31 days *plus* one extra hour the last Sunday of the month when daylight time ends.

How Easter's date is figured

Did you ever wonder how the date for Easter is determined each year?

Easter is always the first Sunday after the first full moon of spring.

That means that Easter can never be earlier than March 22. And it means that Easter can never be later than April 25.

What year came after 1 B.C.?

You could say that one year was skipped in human history.

After the year 1 B.C., calendar measurement immediately went to A.D. 1.

There was no year numbered zero between 1 B.C. and A.D. 1, although in the centuries since, there have been zero years, such as 100, 1800, 1900, etc.

That is why the twenty-first century will technically start in 2001, and not 2000. Since there was no zero year, the first century consisted of the years 1 through 100. The twentieth century consists of the years 1901 through 2000.

However, for practical purposes, people probably will celebrate the new century on January 1, 2000, even though 2000 really belongs to the 100 years of the previous century.

The Fourth of July could be celebrated on July 2 or August 2

The Declaration of Independence wasn't signed on July 4, 1776, as is popularly believed.

Most delegates didn't sign it until August 2.

And there's even confusion whether July 2 or July 4 was the day of declaring independence from England.

The Continental Congress voted for an act of independence on July 2. They passed another vote on July 4 that explained the act.

Some historians place July 2 as the actual date of independence.

Eleven days that never existed

Absolutely nothing happened anywhere in America between September 3 and September 13, 1752.

Nothing happened on those eleven days because they never existed.

America changed its calendar in 1752, and those days were dropped to line up the new calendar.

In 1752, America went from September 2 right to September 14, completely omitting September 3 through 13.

How April Fools' Day began

April Fools' Day started in France in 1564.

Until then, France celebrated New Year's Day on

April 1, but in 1564 their calendar was changed and New Year's was moved to January 1.

Some people continued to celebrate New Year's on April 1, and they were called April Fools. April 1 then became April Fools' Day.

The beginning of Daylight Savings Time

Although Daylight Savings Time was originally proposed by Benjamin Franklin in 1784, it wasn't adopted in the U.S. until 1918.

America wasn't the first country to use daylight time. In 1907, an English builder, William Willett, wanted more time to finish construction jobs by daylight and started campaigning for daylight time, but few people paid any attention to him.

However, with the outbreak of World War I, nations saw the need to conserve electricity. Germany was the first to use daylight time, in 1915. Britain followed in 1916, calling it "Willett Time" in honor of William Willett.

Boxing Day a peaceful holiday

One of the most unusually-named holidays in the world is celebrated in England on December 26. It's called "Boxing Day"—but it has nothing to do with fighting.

Boxing Day is when people in England give boxes of gifts to those who served them during the year.

England has two distinct gift days—Christmas, for gifts to family and friends, and Boxing Day, the day after Christmas, for gifts to others. Boxing Day sounds tough, but it's not.

How days of week got their names

Tuesday, Wednesday, Thursday, and Friday were named after Scandinavian gods.

Tuesday got its name from a god named Tiu, or Tiu's Day; Wednesday from the god Woden, or Woden's Day; Thursday from Thor, or Thor's Day; and Friday from the goddess Fria, or Fria's Day.

Saturday was named for the Roman god Saturn, or Saturn's Day. Sunday was the sun's day, and Monday was originally honored as the moon's day.

Some Christmas facts

Surprisingly, Christmas was *not* a holiday for most Americans until the 1880s.

Before that time, most people worked or went to school on Christmas Day.

It's also surprising to learn that many Puritans in America, and in England, actually banned gift-giving and carol-singing on Christmas, feeling it was anti-religious.

The reason Christmas colors are red and green is because early Christmas tree decorations consisted of red apples on the green tree.

Mother's Day founder not a mother

The founder of Mother's Day, Anna Jarvis, was never a mother herself.

But she created Mother's Day to honor her own mother, who had died May 9, 1905. For years after that, she held memorial services for her mother on the second Sunday of May.

That gave Ms. Jarvis the idea of honoring all mothers, and she wrote hundreds of letters to plead for the observance of Mother's Day.

In May 1913, Pennsylvania made it a holiday, and in 1914, President Wilson proclaimed Mother's Day nationally.

How to avoid 12 o'clock confusion

Should 12 o'clock midnight be called 12 P.M. or 12 A.M.?

And what about 12 o'clock noon?

That's a tough question, and it leads to a lot of confusion. But word experts have an easy solution.

They say you should use neither A.M. nor P.M. after 12 o'clock.

It is, they contend, better to say "12 midnight" and "12 noon"—without any A.M. or P.M.

When you say "12 midnight" or "12 noon," there's no confusion, and it is correct.

How Labor Day began

A member of the United Brotherhood of Carpenters, Peter McGuire, is credited for the idea for Labor Day.

He organized a Labor Day parade in New York City on the first Monday of September in 1882.

Labor Day became a national holiday in 1894 when Congress authorized it. Congress chose the first Monday in September for the annual holiday because that was the day of McGuire's original Labor Day parade.

There won't be another year like 1961 for a long time

1961 was a year that read the same upside down.

That won't happen again for over 4000 years—in 6009.

This man has many birthdays

Probably nobody has had their birthday celebration changed as often as George Washington.

Washington was born on February 11, 1731—but when he was twenty-one years old, the calendar was changed, and February 11 became February 22. For the rest of his life, February 22 was Washington's birthday.

But now, his birthday is usually not celebrated on February 22. It's celebrated on the third Monday in February—and the date changes every year.

The inventor of Christmas cards

One man is credited with inventing Christmas cards.

The idea for sending Christmas cards was started by Sir Henry Cole, who was director of a museum in England in the 1800s.

Cole's hobby was engraving illustrations. One year he sent Christmas illustrations to friends, and put the ones he had left over on sale in a London store.

People quickly bought up the supply, and the next year more were made. That started the Christmas card tradition.

More than 52 weeks in a year

It's always said a year has 52 weeks, but no year has exactly 52 weeks.

A non-leap year has 52 weeks and one extra day.

A leap year has 52 weeks plus two extra days.

No turkey at first Thanksgiving

One of the strangest traditions we practice is eating turkey at Thanksgiving.

It's a strange tradition because according to increasing historical evidence, the Pilgrims—at the first Thanksgiving—did not eat turkey.

Recent research reveals there wasn't a turkey within miles of the Pilgrim's first Thanksgiving.

The main foods were venison, goose, and duck.

You can, of course, enjoy your turkey at Thanksgiving, but just realize that the Pilgrims probably didn't eat any.

Why is it called Mardi Gras?

Mardi Gras is a French term meaning "Fat Tuesday."

It came from the custom of parading a fat ox through the streets of Paris on the Tuesday before Ash Wednesday.

The fat ox symbolized the merrymaking of a meat feast before the fasting required on the next day's onset of Lent.

Those early U.S. citizens didn't have Christmas trees

The custom of having Christmas trees in a home is a relatively new tradition.

Virtually nobody in America had Christmas trees in their homes until the middle of the nineteenth century.

The custom started in Germany, and when Prince Albert of Germany married Queen Victoria of England in 1840, he brought the custom to England and the English-speaking world.

Christmas trees in homes first came to America in about 1850.

Santa Claus was real

Santa Claus is based on a real-life bishop, St. Nicholas, born in the fourth century, in Myra, in Asia Minor.

He was the son of wealthy parents and got a reputation for giving away money and gifts to people in his domain. He came to symbolize gift-giving.

The name Santa Claus is a corruption of St. Nicholas.

Two facts about Friday the 13th

Every year has at least one Friday the 13th. It's impossible to have a year without a Friday the 13th, based on the way our calendars are sequenced.

How do you know which month, or months, have a

Friday the 13th? Any month that starts on a Sunday will have a Friday the 13th.

"Mary Had a Little Lamb" author fights for Thanksgiving

The woman responsible for making Thanksgiving a national holiday was the same woman who wrote the poem "Mary Had a Little Lamb."

She was Sarah Hale.

Before Abraham Lincoln was President, Thanksgiving was not a national holiday.

Mrs. Hale made a personal cause of getting Thanksgiving to be a national holiday, and she was able to convince President Lincoln to make it so.

Why are U.S. presidential elections held in November?

Presidential election day was set years ago when the U.S. was basically a rural, farming country. Congress thought early November was the best time for election day because harvesting was over and winter had not yet made roads impassable.

At any other time, the farmer was either too busy or it was too hard for him to reach the polls.

Anger over " 'Twas the Night Before Christmas"

The man who wrote one of the most popular poems of all time was upset that it was published.

He was Clement Clarke Moore, who wrote "A Visit from St. Nicholas," better known under the title, " 'Twas the Night Before Christmas."

Moore was a teacher and wrote the poem in 1822 for his children.

He was angry when it was made public by a friend in a Troy, New York, newspaper, and surprised when it became so popular.

Some holiday notes

Of all holidays, the one celebrated in most nations of the world is New Year's Day on January 1. The only places it's not celebrated on January 1 are some countries in the Middle East and Asia.

Memorial Day was originally called Decoration Day because of the custom on that day of decorating graves of Civil War veterans.

While Thanksgiving is in November in the United States, it's celebrated on the second Monday in October in Canada.

Why is Easter called Easter? Its name comes from Eostre, the Anglo-Saxon goddess of spring.

Why was Valentine's Day named after St. Valentine?

In the third century, St. Valentine was a bishop in Rome. He married young couples in defiance of a ban by Emperor Claudius II.

Claudius said marriage made poor-quality soldiers, but Valentine continued marriage ceremonies.

Claudius had Valentine beheaded on February 14, 269.

But love triumphed after all. Pope Gelasius declared February 14, 496 as the first Valentine's Day in honor of St. Valentine.

Eighteen

Words & Names

The first chauvinist

The word "chauvinist" comes from a man named Nicholas Chauvin.

He was a military man who served with Napoleon. Chauvin became notorious for stubbornly sticking to a cause in disputes in the French army.

Frisbees named for pie company

Ever wonder where Frisbees got their name?

Frisbees' name comes from the Frisbee Pie Company, of Bridgeport, Connecticut.

The sport of Frisbee-throwing started when pie pans from the Frisbee Company were used by college students in Connecticut.

They started throwing those Frisbee Pie pans around, and the sport's name changed from Frisbee Pie pans to just "Frisbees."

An amazing spelling fact

If you spell out all our numbers, starting with one, two three, four, etc., and keep going all the way up, what's the first number you would come to containing the letter A?

You would not use the letter A until you reach one thousand.

None of the numbers from one through nine-hundred-ninety-nine has an A in it.

The tuxedo named for a town

Ever wonder why a tuxedo is called a tuxedo?

In 1886, a man named Griswold Lorillard designed a new kind of formal suit he could wear to his country club.

That country club was located in a town north of New York City named Tuxedo Park.

Lorillard's new formal suit was popular, and other people copied it. Since it was first worn in Tuxedo Park, it was called then, and forever more, a "tuxedo."

Some facts about words

The word "scuba," as in scuba diving, came from taking the first letters of the name of the equipment—Self-Contained Underwater Breathing Apparatus.

The word "clip" has two exactly opposite meanings—to clasp together, and to cut apart.

Although the abbreviation for the word "ounce" is "oz.," there's no Z in "ounce."

Catgut used in tennis rackets and for strings in musical instruments doesn't come from cats, but from sheep or horses.

Why are white people called Caucasians?

The word "Caucasian" in referring to white people comes from the Caucasus region of Russia.

It was in the Caucasus area that anthropologists found early skulls of ancient white people. The white race was given the name Caucasian.

Ironically, today some Russians, especially in Moscow, refer to people from the Caucasus as "blacks" because of their dark hair.

Awful & artificial were good

Here's an example of how much language can change. An English king once said that a building was "awful" and "artificial"—and he meant that as a compliment.

The word "awful" once meant "awe-inspiring," and the word "artificial" meant "full of art."

Now, those words have exactly the opposite meanings.

Why are the keys on typewriters & computers all mixed up?

Wouldn't it have been easier if all the keys on a typewriter or computer keyboard were in alphabetical order, or fixed so that the letters were in some other more logical order?

The reason the letters are all mixed up in what seems like no logical order goes back to the invention of the typewriter.

In those early machines, letters that were often used together, like Q and U, for example, would jam or stick if they were struck one after the other.

The letters on the keyboard were purposely scattered so the typewriter would work more efficiently.

Efforts to change the keyboard have always met with resistance since then because so many people learned to type on the existing one.

An oddity of the keyboard is that many of the most-used letters, such as E and A, are typed with the left hand, while the majority of people are right-handed.

The person who invented "Hello"

Had it not been for Thomas Edison, people today would probably be answering the telephone by saying "Ahoy" instead of "Hello."

The telephone's inventor, Alexander Graham Bell, thought "Ahoy" was the correct way to answer the phone. Surprisingly, the word "Hello" didn't exist then.

Edison invented the word "Hello" in the 1870s while doing research on clarity of sounds. When the first telephone exchanges opened around the country, Edison campaigned for using "Hello"—and a new word, and custom, were born.

How leftists and rightists got their name

The terms "left" and "right" that we use in politics originated in the French legislature.

In the French National Assembly in the 1700s, liberal delegates seated themselves to the left of the speaker, while the more conservative delegates sat to his right.

That's where the tradition started of referring to people's political views as "left" and "right."

Our alphabet had missing letters

Originally, the English-language alphabet had only 24 letters, and not 26 as we have today.

One missing letter was J, which was the last letter to come into the alphabet.

Before J appeared, the letter I was often used in its place.

The other latecomer to the alphabet was U, often replaced by V in earlier days.

Two-by-fours not really two-by-four

That familiar piece of wood known as a "two-by-four" is *not* two inches by four inches.

Its actual size is one and one half by three and one-half inches.

The reason it's smaller than two-by-four is because of a long-standing custom to measure wood before it's seasoned and planed.

Finished boards are slightly smaller than the name

they're called. Thus, a two-by-four is not quite two-by-four.

Why do we call it guerrilla warfare?

Although it sounds like "gorilla," soldiers who fight in guerrilla wars have nothing to do with gorillas.

The word comes from the Spanish. "Guerrilla" means "little war."

Lobbyists lobbied in real lobby

Ever wonder why people who try to influence politicians are called lobbyists?

The word lobbyist comes from a time when U.S. President Ulysses Grant used to relax each evening in the lobby of the Willard Hotel in Washington.

Those seeking favors used to approach President Grant there. He called them "lobbyists" because they waited for him each night in the lobby.

The bigness of little words

Although some people like to use long words, many of the most important thoughts, biggest ideas, and strongest declarations are expressed in one-syllable words:

Life . . . death . . . hope . . . peace . . . war . . . yes . . . no . . . God . . . love . . . home.

Why do we say computers have a bug in them?

In 1945, a computer at Harvard malfunctioned.

Grace Hopper, who was working with the computer, investigated the problem and found a moth in one of the circuits. She removed the bug with tweezers.

From then on, when something went wrong with a computer, it was said to have a bug in it.

Marathons began in Marathon

The word "marathon" comes from a run once made by a soldier.

It happened in Greece in 490 B.C., when a soldier ran from the town of Marathon to the city of Athens with news of a military victory.

Because his heroic run from Marathon became a memorable event in history, long races today are called marathons—and the distance between Marathon and Athens, a little over twenty-six miles, is the distance of today's marathon races.

How blazers got their name

The jackets we call blazers got their name from a ship.

In the nineteenth century, there was a British ship whose name was *The Blazer*.

The captain of that ship designed special jackets for

his officers. That style of jacket became popular in England—and the style spread elsewhere.

The British called those jackets "blazers" after the ship of the same name—and that's why "blazers" are called "blazers" today.

The story of sideburns

Sideburns got their name from an actual person.

In the nineteenth century, American General Ambrose Burnside made long sideburns popular—except then, they were called "burnsides" after him.

After many years of use, the word "burnside" eventually evolved into "sideburn"—but it's interesting to note that the original word had nothing to do with the side of a face, since the word came from General Burnside's name.

Why are horseshoes considered good luck?

There are several theories about why horseshoes are thought to be lucky, but the main one is that a few hundred years ago, when some people feared witches, these same people thought witches feared horses. That's why witches rode broomsticks instead of horses, according to these people. Therefore, if you put a horseshoe in your house, the sight of it would keep witches away.

People collected horseshoes for luck—and that tradition still exists.

Teddy bears named for U.S. President

It was because of a U.S. President that teddy bears got their name. Teddy bears were named for President Teddy Roosevelt.

Roosevelt went on a well-publicized bear-hunting trip in 1907, about the same time that stuffed animals resembling small bears were first brought on the market.

The stuffed animals were nicknamed "teddy bears" because of Teddy Roosevelt, and the name has continued to this day.

Why U.S. soldiers were called G.I.'s and doughboys

American servicemen, starting in World War II, were called G.I.'s. The initials came from "government issue," describing the uniform and equipment given to them.

But in World War I, American soldiers were called doughboys. That name became popular because soldiers in those days were served so much doughy food.

They don't teach spelling in many countries

In almost all languages except English, most words are spelled as they sound. In English, many words are not.

Therefore, it's necessary to teach spelling in English-speaking countries, but it's less necessary, or not necessary at all, in other countries.

Why the Red Cross is called the Red Cross

The man most responsible for creating the Red Cross was a Swiss banker, Henri Dunant, in 1863.

To honor Dunant's efforts, organizers took his country's flag—which has a white cross on a red background—and got both the name, and symbol, of the Red Cross by reversing the Swiss flag.

Why the number four is unique

Of all our numbers—from one all the way up—only one number has the same number of letters in its name as its meaning.

And that's "four".

All other numbers have a different amount of letters than their meaning.

Amazingly, of the trillions of numbers, only the number four has the same number of letters as the meaning of its name.

Their names became words

The word nicotine came from Jacques Nicot, a French ambassador who imported tobacco plants from America to France.

The magnolia tree was named after Pierre Magnol, a French botanist.

The Jacuzzi got its name from its inventor, Candido Jacuzzi.

Melba toast was named after opera star Nellie Melba, who had it made specially for her.

Leotards were named for Jules Leotard, a French trapeze artist who designed that type of clothing.

Zinnias were named for a German botanist, Gottfried Zinn.

And the Barbie doll was named after a real little girl—Barbie Handler, the daughter of Ruth and Elliot Handler, who were toy manufacturers.

Why A.M. and P.M.?

Although we use the initials A.M. and P.M. for morning and afternoon, many people don't know exactly what those initials stand for.

They're abbreviations for Latin words, *ante meridiem* and *post meridiem*. "Ante" means before, "post" means after, and "meridiem" refers to noon.

What does S.O.S. stand for?

Many people think the distress signal "S.O.S." stands for "Save Our Ship" or "Save Our Souls"—but that's not true.

S.O.S. doesn't stand for anything.

It was chosen as the international distress signal only because those three letters happen to be easy to send by wireless. The letters are formed by three dots, three dashes, and three dots.

The most beautiful words in the English language

A language expert—Wilfred Funk—once published a list of what he thought were the ten most beautiful words in English.

His choices: dawn ... hush ... lullaby ... murmuring ... mist ... luminous ... chimes ... golden ... melody ... and, tranquil.

Why are policemen called cops?

There are several theories on why policemen are called cops, but the one that is thought to be the most plausible is this one:

In the nineteenth century, many policemen wore big copper badges. People then started referring to policemen as "coppers" because you'd always see the big copper badge when a policeman came into view, and people would say, "Here comes a copper."

As time went on, people shortened the word "copper" to "cop."

More facts about words

Illustrations known as silhouettes are named for a French finance minister, Etienne Silhouette, who made silhouettes as a hobby.

Denim got its name from the French town of De Nimes, where it was first made.

The word Gypsy comes from the middle letters of Egypt, since Gypsies were originally thought to be from Egypt.

The word motel—a combination of motor and hotel—was coined by Arthur Heinman, who opened the world's first motel in San Luis Obispo, California, in 1925.

The terms "fat chance" and "slim chance" both mean the same thing.

U.S. might have had a different language

During and after the Revolutionary War, there were some Americans who wanted to break all ties with England, including the use of the English language.

The first Speaker of the House of Representatives, Frederick Muhlenberg, who was of German ancestry, had some discussions about making German the language of the U.S.

Others proposed French, Spanish, Greek, or Hebrew.

As a practical matter, however, since the majority of the U.S. population spoke English, nothing ever came of the idea of switching languages.

How did "trivia" get its name?

The word trivia comes from the Latin *trivium*.

That word literally means "where three roads meet"—or a public square.

In plural, *trivium* becomes *trivia*, which meant "street talk."